Septem

Day by Day with God

Rooting women's lives in the Bible

BRF
Christina Press
Abingdon/Tunbridge Wells

The Bible Reading Fellowship, 15 The Chambers, Vineyard, Abingdon OX14 3FE

First published in Great Britain 2016

ISBN 978 0 85746 399 9

Distributed in Australia by:
Mediacom Education Inc., PO Box 610, Unley, SA 5061.
Tel: 1800 811 311; Fax: 08 8297 8719;
E-mail: admin@mediacom.org.au

Distributed in New Zealand by:
Scripture Union Wholesale, PO Box 760, Wellington
Tel: 04 385 0421; Fax: 04 384 3990;
E-mail: suwholesale@clear.net.nz

Acknowledgements
Scripture quotations taken from The Holy Bible, New International Version (Anglicised edition), copyright © 1979, 1984, 2011 by Biblica. Used by permission of Hodder & Stoughton Publishers, an Hachette UK company. All rights reserved. 'NIV' is a registered trademark of Biblica. UK trademark number 1448790.

Scripture quotations from *The Message*. Copyright © by Eugene H. Peterson 1993, 1994, 1995. Used by permission of NavPress Publishing Group.

Scripture quotations taken from the Holy Bible, New Living Translation, copyright © 1996, 2004, 2007, 2013. Used by permission of Tyndale House Publishers, Inc., Carol Stream, Illinois 60188. All rights reserved.

Scripture taken from The Voice™. Copyright © 2008 by Ecclesia Bible Society. Used by permission. All rights reserved.

Printed by Gutenberg Press, Tarxien, Malta.

Contents

Contributors

Claire Musters is a freelance writer and editor, mum to two gorgeous young children, pastor's wife, worship leader and school governor. Her writing focuses on marriage, parenting, worship, discipleship and issues facing women today.

Christine Platt lives in New Zealand and enjoys the freedom and opportunities that semi-retirement brings. As well as doing local ministry, she travels regularly with teams to East Timor to support the church there in its courageous witness to war-ravaged people.

Alison Teale works as an administrator in tertiary education and has worked as a freelance writer and translator for 20 years.

Jennifer Rees Larcombe runs Beauty from Ashes, an organisation that supports people adjusting to bereavement and trauma.

Tracy Williamson works for MBM Trust, a music and teaching ministry headed up by blind gospel singer Marilyn Baker. Marilyn and Tracy (who is deaf herself) travel the country giving concerts and leading conferences drawing people into wholeness through intimacy with God.

Chris Leonard lives in Surrey with her husband. Their first two grandchildren arrived in 2015 and Chris also remains busy leading creative writing courses and holdays. Her 21st book was published in November 2015.

Lyndall Bywater is married to Phil and lives in Canterbury. She is a freelance writer and speaker, and her favourite subject is prayer.

Sue Rinaldi travels internationally as a worship coordinator, singer-songwriter, communicator, creative consultant and trainer. A regular contributor to magazines and Bible reading notes, she has also written a book called *TREND*.

Diana Archer works as a freelance writer, editor and trainer. She runs the charity Tastelife (www.tastelifeuk.org), set up to help people break free from eating disorders.

Jill Rattle is a retired secondary headteacher living with her husband, Henry, on the south coast of England. She engages with prayer ministry and with individuals seeking spiritual support. She also loves being a grandmother.

Ali Herbert writes...

'The autumn leaves drift by my window...' goes the classic jazz song; and, as we begin our autumn edition of *Day by Day with God*, I am all too aware that summer is quickly receding and soon the winter nights will be drawing in. This season can feel like an ending, as leaves fall, the days get shorter and our warmer clothes get hauled from the back of the wardrobe. Yet it is a time of new beginnings too: a new year starts in educational establishments, and churches get ready for harvest and the joy of Christmas. In *The Message*, John 1:5 says, 'The Life-Light blazed out of the darkness: the darkness couldn't put it out.' It will be great to focus on that 'Life-Light' in these coming months—God's plan of rescue for his beloved world, full of wonder, love and power for each and every one of us.

There's another new beginning for *Day by Day with God*, as I have great joy in introducing you to my co-editor who will work on the commissioning and editing with me. Jill Rattle is a former secondary headteacher, a spiritual counsellor and a contributor to these notes. She is also my mother! It's an unexpected joy to be able to work together to edit this and forthcoming editions.

In this issue we will be looking at how God encourages us with his blazing 'Life-Light' even when we don't feel up to much—even when we would rather snuggle back under the covers on that drizzly November morning and hide away from the world altogether. Gideon and Jonah are great examples of weak people who seemed to be encountering hopeless situations, and yet the Life-Light blazed out for them and brought transformation to their lives and communities.

We begin this issue with Claire Musters' notes on encouragement. It's so important both to be encouraged and to encourage others. Wouldn't it be wonderful if we could be filled with the 'Life-Light' during this season and become known as encouragers to our families and communities?

Jill Rattle writes...

No one has ever given me one of those luxury food hampers (not a hint, Ali!) but that's what these notes have been like, with so many different delights from God's word to savour. I hope you enjoy the riches, too.

Encouragement

Claire Musters writes…

In recent years God has been talking to me about how we all need encouragement. I'm sure part of the reason is that I have a tendency towards negativity and God really wants me to grow out of it, but he has been very gracious to me in the way he has dealt with it. (Being married to someone whose primary 'love language' is words of affirmation has certainly taught me a lot, too.)

I took over the running of our women's ministry in church a few years ago, and I felt that God was asking me to focus mainly on the subject of encouragement. There was just one verse that seemed to sum up what God was calling us to as a group: 'So speak encouraging words to one another. Build up hope so you'll all be together in this, no one left out, no one left behind' (1 Thessalonians 5:11, *The Message*). It has been my hope and prayer, ever since, that we would show love, support, encouragement and unity through the way we interact with one another. When we meet up, I hope we can learn to build one another up intentionally as well as supporting each other in the day-to-day routines of life. My prayer for all of you who are reading these notes is that you will have people around you with whom you can do the same.

In our busy, time-starved society, encouragement can be sadly lacking, but it is vital for the well-being of our souls. There are so many things that can dampen our enthusiasm for life or knock the wind out of our sails, but encouragement is one of the gifts God has given us in order to set the balance right again in our lives. I want to take you on a journey of discovery over the next ten days, delving deeper into the source of all encouragement and revealing how he gently teaches us to be greater encouragers not only of ourselves but of the people around us, too.

Encouraged in order to encourage

Praise be to the God and Father of our Lord Jesus Christ, the Father of compassion and the God of all comfort, who comforts us in all our troubles, so that we can comfort those in any trouble with the comfort we ourselves receive from God. (NIV)

This passage provides an immensely helpful, rounded picture of the role of encouragement in our lives. Paul begins his letter by offering praise to 'the God of all comfort' (v. 3). The word 'comfort' comes from the Greek *parakleseos*, which means 'providing aid', including encouragement.

Paul explains that, just as our suffering can sometimes be because of our faith, so our comfort comes from the source of that faith too. Both he and his companions have suffered greatly, yet it has taught them how to rely on God alone for their hope. That's a lesson that we can continue to learn throughout our lives. I can be exceedingly quick to get into self-sufficiency mode when faced with pressures and difficulties. Sometimes, I remember to lean on God only once I've exhausted my own resources, which is not how God intends us to live.

The latest season in my life has included some fairly big difficulties, which have threatened to floor me, but I've really experienced God's care and comfort. Already, just sharing with others has opened up a sense of encouragement and support—not only for myself but as an offering to others, too. That is how God wants us to live—coming to him for our encouragement and then reaching out to those around us. When we allow him to fashion and mould us through our difficulties, we can help the people we meet, at a later date, who are going through similar experiences.

Just being able to shout encouragement from the sidelines, revealing that we've made it through to the other side of the issue they are struggling with, is such a gift—both for the recipient and the one who gives the support.

Have you considered the cycle of encouragement before today? Thank God that he ministers his comfort to us and gives us opportunities to give out to others what we have received.

CLAIRE MUSTERS

The ultimate encourager

[Jesus said] 'The Advocate, the Holy Spirit, whom the Father will send in my name, will teach you all things and will remind you of everything I have said to you. Peace I leave with you; my peace I give you.' (NIV)

As we saw yesterday, it is vital to remember that God is the one who offers us comfort and encouragement. As Psalm 10:17 says, 'You, Lord, hear the desire of the afflicted; you encourage them, and you listen to their cry.' I can't imagine how the disciples must have felt during this, their final meal shared with Jesus, but I think I would have been feeling very lost when he explained that he would soon be leaving. However, Jesus revealed that it was actually better for him to go, in order that the ultimate *paraclete* (comforter, encourager, helper) could be sent to dwell with believers for all time. (Indeed, in John 14:12, Jesus had said that anyone who believed in him would do greater things than him, because he was going to the Father.)

It is an amazing fact that the Holy Spirit is the promised Comforter who reveals the truth of God to our hearts and encourages us from within, even in the midst of difficulties. In this passage Jesus unveils the wonderful mystery of what life as a believer truly means: the Holy Spirit lives within us, so he is with us constantly. Jesus is in the Father, we are in Jesus, and Jesus, by his Spirit, is within us. Just focusing on the truths contained in his words can really encourage our spirits.

If we are honest, there are times when we all feel alone, lost or even despairing, yet we have the reminder here that the Spirit of Jesus dwells within us. His specific reason for being there is to be our adviser, the one who reminds us of God's words, to provide us with peace and to be our ultimate encourager.

Holy Spirit, how amazing it is to have your constant encouragement coming from within. Help me to be attentive to your whisperings.

CLAIRE MUSTERS

Encouraging yourself in God

David was greatly distressed because the men were talking of stoning him; each one was bitter in spirit because of his sons and daughters. But David found strength in the Lord his God. (NIV)

Encouragement gives us fresh hope, as well as the courage to carry on. David is a great biblical character to show us how to find encouragement in God. As we read in 1 Samuel 27, 29 and 30, he decided to escape King Saul's pursuit of him and went to live within the Philistines' land. He ended up serving a Philistine king, which must have been bizarre for them all (as he had previously killed the Philistine giant Goliath). Indeed, not all of the king's men accepted him and eventually David and his men were sent back to Ziklag, where their wives and children had been living. With the men absent, Amalekites had raided the village and taken their women and children captive.

At this point, David's men began to turn on him—but what was David's response? He didn't despair, run or try to plead with them: we are told that he 'found strength in the Lord' and then asked for the ephod so that he could ask God what to do.

How did he encourage himself in God? It isn't spelt out in scripture, but, given what is revealed about him in the psalms he penned, I think he probably brought to mind past examples of God's faithfulness and stood firm on God's promises. A look through Psalms 34—41, for example, shows that David wasn't afraid to be honest about his circumstances and emotions, yet he always turned to praise, reminding himself how trustworthy and faithful God is.

I love the tone of Psalm 37, where it seems as if David is revealing what he has learned over the years: 'I was young and now I am old, yet I have never seen the righteous forsaken' (v. 25). In other psalms he tells his downcast soul to look to God.

Spend some time thinking about ways that you can encourage yourself in God today.

CLAIRE MUSTERS

Becoming an encourager

Those who are led by the Spirit of God are children of God. The Spirit you received doesn't make you slaves. Otherwise you would live in fear again. Instead, the Holy Spirit you received made you God's adopted child. (NIRV)

You may be thinking that it's all very well to talk about receiving and giving encouragement, but actually you find it quite hard to do. I don't think you are alone, and there can be various reasons for the difficulty. For example, some of us have a natural tendency to be anxious, negative or insecure, so that it is hard for us to lift our heads above our problems. It is easy to accept these natural tendencies, telling ourselves that it is simply the way we were born. However, Romans 8 is full of truth for any of us who struggle with the concept of encouragement.

First, there is no longer any condemnation for us (v. 1), so we don't need to take on negative thinking about how badly we've given or received encouragement in the past. Verse 2 says that we are set free in Christ: the Holy Spirit reminds us that we are now children of God. We no longer have to live by our sinful nature.

I know that trying to put off our old nature and put on the new, in our own strength, can be frustrating. In fact, it's impossible, but the good news is that we have the Holy Spirit's help. With his help, we *can* change. Those who tend to be negative and critical can be encouraging and positive. Those who allow their thoughts to spiral downwards and end up being self-absorbed in the midst of difficulties can lift their heads and receive comfort and help from the Father.

Our passage for today also includes the amazing promise that God is working for our good in all things (v. 28). What an encouragement to cling to!

Lord, I am sorry for the times when I seem to be more at home with my old nature. Help me to set it aside and learn how to be an encourager.

CLAIRE MUSTERS

Be each other's fan club

Do not let any unwholesome talk come out of your mouths, but only what is helpful for building others up according to their needs, that it may benefit those who listen. (NIV)

This chapter in Paul's letter to the Ephesians is focused on unity, with every believer playing the part that God has called them to. This idea follows on from yesterday's reading about putting off the old self and living in the way of the Spirit. It is interesting that verse 29 zooms in on our speech and how we should use it intentionally for the building up of the people around us. We certainly need encouragement from one another—perhaps more so than at any other time in history. There are more people suffering from depression than ever before: 85,000 deaths worldwide occur each year due to depression.

We each desperately need people who are rooting for us. Gary Chapman, renowned marriage counsellor and author of the bestselling book *The 5 Love Languages*, recognises how much difference it makes in a person's life. Indeed, in his book *The Family You've Always Wanted* he writes, 'From the smallest child to the oldest adult, when our fan club applauds us, we try harder.'

As we have seen, we have a responsibility to live as children of God, not by our old sinful nature. We don't have to strive to do it in our own strength, as we have the Holy Spirit's help. However, as Ephesians 4 reminds us, we are have been made part of God's family, his body, with his Son at the head. Verse 16 says, 'From him the whole body, joined and held together by every supporting ligament, grows and builds itself up in love.' Note the imagery: we each make up a part of the supporting framework of the body. We need one another's support and encouragement. We are not meant to journey in this life alone, but alongside others who will spur us on to be the best we can be.

Do you have people in your life who encourage you? If so, find a way to thank them today. If not, ask God to bring encouragers into your life.

CLAIRE MUSTERS

The power of the tongue

The tongue is a small part of the body, but it makes great boasts. Consider what a great forest is set on fire by a small spark. The tongue also is a fire. (NIV)

Yesterday we looked at how important it is to have people who spur us on. One of the obvious ways in which we can give encouragement is through what we say, but how often do we actively think about the ratio of positive and negative words that come out of our mouths? So often we speak without thinking (I know I do!), and today's passage reminds us of the power our words hold.

James uses incredibly vivid imagery, comparing the tongue to the rudder on a ship or the small spark of fire that eventually destroys a forest. It might be a tiny part of our bodies, but it truly can control us. James ends with a challenge: our mouths should not be bringing forth both praise to God and negativity towards others.

We could feel condemned after reading what James has to say. All of us can surely think of someone who is constantly negative and cutting—and what a terrible atmosphere they create in a room. We have a choice about what comes out of our mouths.

The tongue is a powerful instrument, but Proverbs 18:21 reminds us that it 'has the power of life and death'. So not only can the words we say destroy a person; they can also build a person up. How important it is to use our tongues to speak out encouragement! Sometimes we assume that if someone is doing well, they don't need our positive words, yet R.T. Kendall admits in his book *Your Words have Power* that he still needs affirmation each time he preaches. He experienced first-hand, too, that even the great preacher Martyn Lloyd-Jones needed it. It is a universal truth that we all thrive under encouragement.

If, like me, you find that giving words of encouragement doesn't come naturally, spend some time practising today. Choose a couple of people and speak something encouraging to them.

CLAIRE MUSTERS

The words that bring life

But because of his great love for us, God, who is rich in mercy, made us alive with Christ even when we were dead in transgressions—it is by grace you have been saved. (NIV)

We have talked over the past few days about giving words of encouragement. They can simply be words of thanks when something goes well or when somebody's actions are a real blessing to us, but the greatest words of encouragement that we can give and receive are the truths about our identity in Christ. A quick word to someone who is having a bad day, reminding them that they are God's child, loved and accepted and full of his Spirit, can do wonders to affirm them.

It is important that we regularly remind ourselves, too, of who we are in Christ. That is why I have chosen this passage in Ephesians. It is stuffed full of truth about what our identity is, now that we are in Christ. Here are some of the highlights! We were once dead in our sin but we are now alive. God has seated us next to Jesus. We have this gift through grace: we don't deserve it and it is ours not because of anything we have done or need to do. We were once far away but are now near God. Jesus is our peace. We are now citizens of heaven and members of God's household, part of his body in which the Holy Spirit dwells.

Isn't that all amazing? To top it off, the previous chapter of Ephesians reminds us that we are not just part of God's household; we are children of God: 'He destined us for adoption as his children through Jesus Christ, according to the good pleasure of his will' (1:5, NRSV). I don't know about you, but soaking in those truths really lifts my spirit.

Lord, I thank you so much for the new life that I have in Jesus; for the standing and authority that you have lavished upon me because of him. I stand in amazement before you today.

CLAIRE MUSTERS

Developing a positive thought life

Finally, brothers and sisters, whatever is true, whatever is noble, whatever is right, whatever is pure, whatever is lovely, whatever is admirable—if anything is excellent or praiseworthy—think about such things. (NIV)

This passage is such a helpful key to living our lives well. In it we are told how important it is to have an attitude of rejoicing (and this from a man in prison). Paul also says that we should not worry, but should bring all our concerns to God, and this process will allow our minds and hearts to be full of his peace.

It is vital that we develop a positive thought life, by immersing ourselves in the word of God and praying regularly. We've already seen how David did this—but it is, of course, a process, not an instant fix. Just think what a minefield our minds can be! Often it is the thoughts we mull over that cause us to become discouraged. Romans 12:2 combats this effect, telling us, 'Be transformed by the renewing of your mind.' How do we do that? Well, in 2 Corinthians 10:5 we are told to 'take captive every thought to make it obedient to Christ'. This is a very active thing: we need to fight for our mind and boot out any thoughts that are not helpful. The same verse begins by saying, 'We demolish arguments and every pretension that sets itself up against the knowledge of God': these are the negative influences that can come up against us in our minds.

The words of Philippians 4:8 (quoted above) can be truly life-changing. I'd encourage you to write them out and place them where you will see them regularly. They are a great plumb-line to use throughout your day, as you stop and think every so often about what kinds of thoughts you've allowed yourself to dwell on. You'll probably be shocked by some of the things your mind entertains without you really noticing; I was when I tried it!

Lord I am sorry that I sometimes allow all sorts of thoughts to linger in my mind, unchallenged. Help me to be proactive about throwing out the unhelpful thoughts and replacing them with those that do me good.

CLAIRE MUSTERS

Choose to speak and act positively

For the kingdom of God is not a matter of eating and drinking, but of righteousness, peace and joy in the Holy Spirit… Let us therefore make every effort to do what leads to peace and to mutual edification. (NIV)

When you act and speak, you make a series of (often subconscious) choices. Romans 14 encourages us not to make ourselves a stumbling block to those who think differently from us (or are perhaps 'weaker' in their faith). Paul was referencing some of the disputes that occurred in the early church. Some believers, for example, felt free to eat anything, including all kinds of meat from the marketplaces. Others ate only vegetables because they were worried that they might unknowingly eat meat that had been sacrificed to idols; often, these sacrifices were only partially burned and the rest of the meat was sent to market to be sold.

While some believers were free from any sense of guilt because they knew that idols were worthless and unreal anyway, others (possibly those who had previously been idol worshippers) found it unhelpful to see their fellow Christians eating this meat freely. What we can learn from this is that we should not be judgemental or critical of others; rather, we should be aware that what we do and say affects the people around us, and we should seek always to build them up.

Church can be full of critical comparisons, even though this is the last place where it should happen. Try to keep a check on any subtle criticisms you may engage in! Of course we need to be honest; life is full of problems and, as Christians, we are not immune to them. If we're not careful, though, all we will see are the problems. Even when we think we are empathising with someone, we have a tendency to join in with negativity rather than lifting the conversation to more positive words of hope and encouragement. Proverbs 10:11 reminds us that 'the mouth of the righteous is a fountain of life', so let's use ours in that way.

Lord, help me not to be a stumbling block to anyone around me, but to be someone who encourages and builds up others. Teach me to keep a check on the words I say and the actions I take.

CLAIRE MUSTERS

Encouraging each other

Let's keep a firm grip on the promises that keep us going. He always keeps his word. Let's see how inventive we can be in encouraging love and helping out, not avoiding worshipping together as some do but spurring each other on. (*The Message*)

On the final day of this set of notes, let's remind ourselves that God calls us to journey together in order to encourage each other in our walk with God—to keep going even when it gets tough. The examples in today's passage are fairly extreme. They describe friends being thrown in prison and enemies seizing belongings—and yet the believers all stuck together through the hard times as well as the easier ones.

I love the encouraging language used in *The Message* version of this passage from Hebrews: 'Let's see how inventive we can be in encouraging love and helping out.' It speaks to me of God's creativity—that there are so many new and inventive ways we can find to be encouraging to one another.

That's the challenge I'd like to leave you with, along with the prayer found in 2 Thessalonians 2:16–17: 'May our Lord Jesus Christ himself and God our Father, who loved us and by his grace gave us eternal encouragement and good hope, encourage your hearts and strengthen you in every good deed and word' (NIV).

I do pray that you have gained encouragement from these notes and have experienced in an even deeper way how God strengthens us through the work of his Son and the Holy Spirit, in order that we may be strong in our faith and reach out to those around us. Like David and Paul, let us continue to find our encouragement in God and champion the people he has brought into our lives, helping them to do the same.

Thank you, Lord, that you are the source of all encouragement. Help me to draw on you even more deeply. You also set us in families and churches so that we can build one another up: thank you.

CLAIRE MUSTERS

Gideon

Christine Platt writes...

The Israelites in Old Testament times could look back at the tremendous love that God had shown them—rescuing them from slavery in Egypt, appearing on Mount Sinai and giving them the law, providing manna, water and quail for 40 years in the desert and finally granting them a victory march into the promised land under Joshua's leadership. This was the culmination of God's covenant promises given to their revered ancestors—Abraham, Isaac and Jacob.

You'd think that nothing would stop them from joyously taking possession of the land from the Canaanites and establishing God's kingdom on earth. All started well: 'The people served the Lord throughout the lifetime of Joshua and of the elders who outlived him' (Judges 2:7, NIV). Sadly, the rot soon set in: 'Another generation grew up who knew neither the Lord nor what he had done for Israel... They forsook the Lord... and worshipped various gods of the people around them' (2:10, 12).

What happened? Did the people not teach their children about the awesome power and faithfulness of God? Maybe the children didn't want to know?

God did not stand idly by or allow his kingdom to fail. He used tough love. He allowed foreign armies to oppress his people until they were so desperate that they cried out to him for help. He sent a succession of judges (leaders) to rescue them, the five main ones being Ehud, Deborah, Gideon, Jephthah and Samson. The depressing cycle that recurs throughout Judges is of disobedience, oppression, distress and rescue. With some relief we note that, despite Israel's repeated failures, God kept his covenant and demonstrated his vast unending patience with his deeply flawed people. The covenant now extends not only to all Jewish people but also to all Gentiles (Ephesians 2:11–22). Such is the love of our majestic God!

To set the scene for Gideon: Judge Deborah and her army general, Barak, won a resounding victory over the Canaanites and the land had peace for 40 years. Unfortunately, though, the Israelites couldn't keep their eyes off foreign gods. They 'did evil in the eyes of the Lord', so an enemy, Midian, came to draw them back to their true king. The Midianites oppressed the Israelites for seven years, until an unlikely hero arose—Gideon. His story is an inspiration to all other unlikely heroes and heroines, including us.

Who are you listening to?

'This is what the Lord, the God of Israel, says: I brought you up out of Egypt, out of the land of slavery... I said to you, "I am the Lord your God; do not worship the gods of the Amorites, in whose land you live." But you have not listened to me.' (NIV)

The Israelites' hold on the land was tenuous. Their enemies freely invaded, stealing their crops and livestock while the Israelites cowered in caves, utterly defeated. Yet, these were God's chosen people. Where were their faith and victory? As crazy as it seems, instead of trusting the God who had done mighty miracles for them, they were trusting in idols that were clearly letting them down. It took seven years for them to remember that their king was God, not one of the local deities.

God's instructions had been clear: 'I am the Lord your God... You shall have no other gods before me' (Exodus 20:2–3). But the Israelites weren't listening.

Are we listening to him? Do enemies come in and rob us of our rightful inheritance—peace, love, joy and victory? Have we forgotten what God has done for us in the past? Do our problems seem insurmountable? We can be certain that wherever God's people are seeking to live with passionate energy for him, there will be enemies who try to deflect, discourage, disable and deter.

At those times we need to be listening, really listening, to the one who has the answers. The problems may look huge, but God is vastly more huge. As believers we have a massive advantage over the Israelites. We have God's Holy Spirit within to prompt us to trust God and follow him wholeheartedly, to guide us in the right paths and to help us identify any idols that try to worm their way into our lives. We need to learn from the Israelites' mistakes and keep remembering and listening.

Make a list of situations in which God has helped you in the past. Use it to bolster your faith as you face the challenges of this day.

CHRISTINE PLATT

The workplace meeting

The angel of the Lord came and sat down... Gideon was threshing wheat... He said, 'The Lord is with you, mighty warrior.' 'Pardon me, my Lord,' Gideon replied, 'but if the Lord is with us, why has all this happened to us?' (NIV)

It was just another tedious day, living in fear of enemies coming to steal the family's food. Gideon didn't have much to look forward to that day. His expectations were low. All he hoped for was to thresh his wheat in peace, so that it could be ground into flour to feed his family. He didn't seem surprised that an angel came to visit him at work. Maybe he was so demoralised by constant oppression that nothing could stir him any more. He was certainly in no state of mind to be sent out as a 'mighty warrior'.

It is deeply encouraging to me that God sometimes chooses to use the most insignificant among us. Yes, he does use highly gifted people, but also those who are ordinary. The apostle Paul writes to the people of Corinth, 'Not many of you were wise by human standards; not many were influential; not many were of noble birth. But God chose the foolish things of the world... God chose the weak... the lowly... and the despised things... so that no one may boast before him' (1 Corinthians 1:26–29). David was the youngest in his family, yet he rose to become the greatest king Israel ever had.

It's intriguing that Gideon had his divine encounter in his workplace, not in a 'holy' place of prayer; not at a time when he might have been concentrating on seeking God, but when he was doing his everyday activities. As we will discover, that meeting sent Gideon's life off on a completely unexpected trajectory and brought deliverance to the nation.

God can empower the seemingly insignificant among us to accomplish his great purposes for our families, friends, neighbours, nation and world. Let's be ready for him to visit, wherever we are.

Lord, here I am. I'm an ordinary person, but you are extraordinary and can equip ordinary people. Help me to recognise and respond in faith to your call, wherever and whenever it comes.

CHRISTINE PLATT

A drastic change of heart

The men of the town demanded of Joash, 'Bring out your son. He must die, because he has broken down Baal's altar…' But Joash replied to the hostile crowd around him, '… If Baal really is a god, he can defend himself when someone breaks down his altar.' (NIV)

Gideon's first assignment for God was daunting. His father, Joash, worshipped idols. Joash had an altar to Baal and a pole symbolising the goddess Asherah. Gideon's task was to demolish both altar and pole and sacrifice his father's bull on an altar dedicated to God. Surrounded by idol-worshipping neighbours, no wonder Gideon was scared and did the deed at night. All the same, he did it, knowing that the consequences would be hostility and possible death, even at the hand of his own father.

Surprise, surprise! Joash defended his son's actions. What a shock for Joash to wake up in the morning and see his Baal altar demolished and his precious bull smouldering on an altar to the God of Israel. Maybe the Lord spoke to his heart in that moment and he repented and turned back to worship the living God.

Gideon was God's man, and God was not going to let any hostile mob kill him. Of course, Gideon didn't know how it would turn out. Nor can we predict the consequences of our actions. Sometimes God does not rescue, as in the case of the Christian martyrs killed by the forces of ISIS in Syria.

Whenever we stand up for God and his values, there will be some who support us and some who oppose. Probably, for many of us, the opposition will not involve death threats, but, more likely, scorn and rejection. There will be some people who hear God speaking when they see courageous actions and will have a drastic change of heart, as Joash did. For example, if we support education about biblical values in schools or speak out against abortion or euthanasia on demand, there will be vociferous opposition, but some will be glad that there is a voice speaking out for God.

In these situations, whatever we say needs to be offered with gentleness and humility. 'A gentle response defuses anger, but a sharp tongue kindles a temper-fire' (Proverbs 15:1, The Message).

CHRISTINE PLATT

God hears and answers prayer

Gideon said to God, 'If you will save Israel by my hand as you have promised—look, I will place a wool fleece on the threshing-floor. If there is dew only on the fleece and all the ground is dry, then I will know that you will save Israel by my hand.' (NIV)

Israel's enemies poured into the Jezreel Valley anticipating an easy victory. In the past, the Israelites had taken one look at the hordes coming against them and fled to hide in caves, leaving their fields and livestock to be gathered as plunder. This time, though, their enemies were in for a shock.

What made the Israelites respond to Gideon's trumpet call and become brave enough to confront their enemies? Somehow they knew that God's Spirit had come upon Gideon (v. 34). At last there was someone to lead them to victory.

The Israelites seemed to have more confidence in Gideon's calling than he did. He brought his doubts and fears to God, needing two boosts to his faith. Just imagine Gideon's trepidation as he got up in the early morning, went to investigate the fleece and found it sopping wet! It was a real God-moment, but he needed even more reassurance and wasn't afraid to ask. God showed Gideon that he had listened to him and understood his human weakness, by responding in power and patience with the miracles of the dew.

Gideon's prayer was humble, honest and specific. As believers, we have the same Holy Spirit, who will guide us how to pray for ourselves and others and can also help us discover God's will for our daily lives. 'God bless my family' is a vague prayer: how will you know when it is answered? Let's learn from Gideon and make specific and measurable requests to God. Gideon's prayers were answered rapidly. We may have to wait sometimes, but there is no need to lose heart. God is listening and he will answer, with his perfect timing.

Ask the Holy Spirit to guide you about specific things you can pray for right now. Make a list and be sure to tell others and give thanks to God when the answers come.

CHRISTINE PLATT

March on, my soul, be strong

The Midianites, the Amalekites and all the other eastern peoples had settled in the valley, thick as locusts. Their camels could no more be counted than the sand on the seashore. (NIV)

Deborah, the previous judge in Israel, sang a song when her army won a decisive victory. One phrase leaps to my attention: 'March on, my soul, be strong' (Judges 5:21). Deborah certainly exemplified that courage and conviction. Army language has gone out of fashion in parts of today's church, but as a child I used to sing, 'Onward Christian soldiers, marching as to war' (Sabine Baring-Gould).

I wonder if we need to recapture that indomitable spirit of faith when we're confronted with problems in our world, like secular and atheistic philosophies, violent fundamentalism, hungry children, desperate refugees, family violence and child abuse. What can we learn from Gideon's experience about how to face these issues?

From Gideon's story we learn that God does not require thousands of soldiers or the latest weapons of mass destruction to accomplish his purposes. He requires obedient and faithful people who are willing to step out and risk all for him. As a military tactic, it was absurd to send most of Gideon's army home, but God wanted to make a point—to remind the Israelites that he was their commander-in-chief, so they should follow his guidance. In no way would they be able to boast about their magnificent victory. It would be all God's doing. A tiny force plus God was more than equal to the task.

It may be that you are facing a battle of gigantic proportions in your personal or family life: 'March on, be strong!' Remember what God has done in the past. Many 'giants' oppose God and his rule in our world today. Let's 'march on and be strong' and play our part in the confidence of God's ultimate victory.

Almighty God, forgive me when the difficulties seem too huge and I give up. Help me, as your foot soldier, to trust you for victory, no matter how powerless and small I feel.

CHRISTINE PLATT

Use your weapons wisely

Dividing the three hundred men into three companies, [Gideon] placed trumpets and empty jars in the hands of all of them, with torches inside. 'Watch me,' he told them. 'Follow my lead.' (NIV)

The weapons that Gideon's 300-strong force used for the initial battle were empty jars, trumpets and torches. These soldiers were virtually defenceless against even a tiny proportion of their enemies. They couldn't just stand on the hill and hope for the best. They had to use what they had—smashing the jars, blowing the trumpets, holding the torches high and shouting at the top of their voices—all at the right time.

Their real power was not in the loudness of the trumpets but in their evident faith in God. If he didn't intervene, they would be utterly lost. God created chaos in the Midianite camp and the enemy soldiers destroyed each other while Gideon and each of his men held their position (v. 22). I find that an inspiring image of boldness and trust. The Israelites were doing their part and watching while God worked on their behalf.

God has given us weapons, too. Again, they are not the most obvious means of victory. Instead of empty jars, we have his word and prayer. 'God's word is an indispensable weapon. In the same way, prayer is essential in this ongoing warfare' (Ephesians 6:17–18, *The Message*). Praying scripture combines these two powerful forces into one mighty burst of energy.

I wish I could say I was a faithful prayer warrior, but I often need the stimulus of praying with others to keep me on track. I suspect that if I spent all my 'worry time' in scripture-based prayer, my life and ministry would be radically different. On occasion I have been privileged to watch while God has done his wonderful work in answer to my prayer: they have been awe-inspiring moments. God has given us all we need to see changes in our own lives as well as others' lives. His weapons are effective and powerful.

Choose some scripture verses to pray regularly into your own life and into any problems you see around you. Join a prayer group if that helps. Be alert and watch for God to answer.

CHRISTINE PLATT

Soothing arguments

Now the Ephraimites asked Gideon, 'Why have you treated us like this? Why didn't you call us when you went to fight Midian?' And they criticised him sharply. (NIV 1984)

It's an unfortunate fact of life that, no matter what you do, there will always be some people who complain. To find fault seems to come much easier than looking for the positives in a situation.

The Israelites were experiencing success on the battlefield for the first time in years. It must have been a heady moment to see their tormentors running away in panic, but those from the tribe of Ephraim decided to moan. Instead of coming to Gideon with thanks and heartfelt appreciation for their change in fortune, they criticised him for not including them in the first part of the battle. It was actually God who had whittled down the Israelite army and Gideon could have justified himself on that accusation.

We could hardly have blamed Gideon for getting impatient and angry with them, but the Spirit of God was still on him and he answered with humility and wisdom (vv. 2–3). We are told, 'At this their resentment against him subsided.'

Criticism can come when we least expect it and can catch us off-guard. It's easy then for tempers to flare. Unjustified criticism is especially hard to take. I've come to the conclusion that no amount of arguing helps. Often, people are unwilling to listen to any viewpoint other than their own. In a recent altercation I ended up saying, 'I'm sorry you think that I hurt you. Can we put this behind us and move on?' It wasn't very satisfactory, but it did prove to be a way forward.

Gideon's response was much wiser and more effective. God will enable us to work towards a peaceful resolution even with the most argumentative of people. 'A gentle answer turns away wrath, but a harsh word stirs up anger' (Proverbs 15:1).

Do you find yourself often complaining? Try to look for the positives. If you're being unjustly criticised, seek God for a response that will make the resentment subside rather than inflame it.

CHRISTINE PLATT

Persevere to the end

Gideon and his three hundred men, exhausted yet keeping up the pursuit, came to the Jordan and crossed it. He said to the men of Sukkoth, 'Give my troops some bread; they are worn out, and I am still pursuing Zebah and Zalmunna, the kings of Midian.' (NIV)

You have to admire the tenacity and loyalty of Gideon's 300 men. With puny weapons, they had courageously taken on an overwhelming force. They'd seen God act mightily on their behalf. They could have thought they'd earned a break, but no, they pursued the fleeing enemy. God had promised Gideon that he would strike down all the Midianites (6:16).

Exhausted and hungry, the soldiers came to two towns where they expected to find help with food and supplies, but they were refused point-blank. Were some of them tempted to give up at that point? I might have been. I might well have bleated, 'It's too hard', but they were made of sterner stuff and all continued on until they routed the whole army (v. 12). They finished the job they had set out to do.

The writer to the Hebrews reminds us that we also have a job to do: 'Let us throw off everything that hinders and the sin that so easily entangles. And let us run with perseverance the race marked out for us, fixing our eyes on Jesus… [who] endured the cross' (Hebrews 12:1–2). Jesus persevered despite all the opposition the enemy could throw at him.

Gideon's soldiers had the vivid experience of seeing God confuse the Midianite army to motivate them onwards, as well as having Gideon ahead of them as their leader. We have the magnificent person of Jesus to spur us on when we're tempted to flag or even give up on our faith journey. The key is to fix our eyes on our majestic leader and get rid of any hindrances—activities, habits or attitudes—that might deflect us, remembering also the countless millions of faithful men and women who have blazed the trail before us (Hebrews 12:1).

Lord Jesus, you didn't allow any opposition to turn you away from wholehearted obedience to your Father's will. Help me to fix my eyes on you. Show me anything that is a hindrance to my relationship with you.

CHRISTINE PLATT

Be careful what you sow

Then [Gideon] asked Zebah and Zalmunna, 'What kind of men did you kill at Tabor? 'Men like you,' they answered, 'each one with the bearing of a prince.' Gideon replied, 'Those were my brothers... As surely as the Lord lives, if you had spared their lives, I would not kill you.' (NIV)

Those of us who've never experienced war probably find this passage disturbing. Let's try to look beyond the bloodshed and see what spiritual truths we can glean.

Even though Zebah and Zalmunna were avowed enemies of the Israelites, Gideon would have shown them mercy if they'd been merciful to his brothers. The enemy kings reaped what they had sown. The towns that had refused to feed Gideon's army also reaped what they had sown. Ignoring the needs of others, they brought suffering upon themselves. Against the backdrop of all this angst, this is the truth that remains solid: you reap what you sow. We see it in the natural world. If you make the effort to plant tomatoes, you'll get a crop; if you're lazy and the ground is left barren, you'll only get weeds.

This is how Paul explains it: 'The person who plants selfishness, ignoring the needs of others—ignoring God!—harvests a crop of weeds... But the one who plants in response to God... harvests a crop of real life, eternal life... So let's not allow ourselves to get fatigued doing good... Right now... let us work for the benefit of all, starting with the people closest to us in the community of faith.' (Galatians 6:7–10, *The Message*).

Sometimes it seems that we keep doing good and no one appreciates it. We sow a lot but reap little in the human sense. That's an unfortunate reality in our world today, but we know that God appreciates our work. He takes note of all our efforts to serve others and he will reward us in his time. The alternative is deadly to life: if we are mean to people and refuse to offer forgiveness or other help, our spiritual vitality will wither.

Be on the alert today for any way you can help others. Do it for Jesus' sake, not for any human affirmation. If you do receive thanks, so much the better!

CHRISTINE PLATT

A fatal error

Gideon made the gold into an ephod, which he placed in Ophrah, his town. All Israel prostituted themselves by worshipping it there, and it became a snare to Gideon and his family. (NIV)

Have you ever had a fantastic idea that turned sour on you? The Israelites welcomed Gideon back as a conquering hero. They forgot that God himself had given the victory. In consequence they wanted to make Gideon their king. He was too smart to fall for that temptation and reminded them that 'the Lord will rule over you' (v.23). Good man!

He then seems to have had a complete brain fade. What was he thinking? He asked for a donation and got 50lb of gold, but it proved to be his downfall. He could have used that wealth to do constructive things for his people. Money is an enabling asset when wisely used. In making a priestly ephod—a sleeveless garment worn by the high priest—was Gideon claiming to be a spiritual leader in Israel? God had called him to be a military leader, not a spiritual one.

Gideon's father had been the custodian of an altar to Baal. Now Gideon was the custodian of this golden ephod in his own home town. People came to believe that the ephod represented victory and, again, forgot God. Even Gideon was drawn to it rather than to the God who had appeared to him at the threshing floor and led him to victory. How quickly we forget our Maker and put our trust in human or worldly things!

The ephod project sounded wonderfully spiritual but it had the seeds of death in it. Gideon had not thought through all the implications of his actions. Ultimately his good work was undone by that fatal error.

Jesus, in the situations I face in my family, at work and in my personal life, help me to think clearly and review all the possible outcomes, so that my decisions don't become a snare to me or to others.

CHRISTINE PLATT

The snare of success

The land had peace for forty years. Jerub-Baal son of Joash [Gideon] went back home to live. He had seventy sons of his own, for he had many wives. His concubine, who lived in Shechem, also bore him a son, whom he named Abimelek. (NIV)

After all these tumultuous events, Gideon—now known as Jerub-Baal ('Let Baal contend'), having chopped up Baal's altar—retired to his home town. He seems to have rather lost the plot in terms of family life, though. Did his success go to his head? He had many wives, 70 sons and a concubine—a bit excessive! Polygamy was tolerated in Israel but it was never authorised by God. Maybe Gideon's outstanding military successes and the adulation of the people led him to think he deserved to live like a king.

When God entrusts success to any human being, he knows that it can go one of two ways. Either they will increasingly recognise that all their gifts and skills come from God and will become more dependent on God's guidance and enabling, or the opposite will happen. They will forget God and think they really are amazingly capable individuals who've achieved at the highest level all on their own.

Some people, like King David, who was king during Israel's golden era, veer from one extreme to the other. He excelled in demonstrating a humble, thankful heart towards God. Then, in his relationship with Bathsheba, he decided he could break all the rules and get away with it (2 Samuel 11—12). God promptly brought his servant down to earth with a bump and, to his credit, David repented of his errors.

It is said that success is harder to cope with than failure. Difficulties tend to compel us back to God, whereas Satan can use success to entice us to delusional self-belief and a sense of entitlement. How do you handle success in your own life?

Mighty Saviour, all I have comes from you—life, a relationship with you, gifts and talents. I want to use them all for your honour. 'Not to us, Lord… but to your name be the glory' (Psalm 115:1).

CHRISTINE PLATT

Grasping for power

Abimelek son of Jerub-Baal went to his mother's brothers in Shechem and said to them and to all his mother's clan, 'Which is better for you: to have all seventy of Jerub-Baal's sons rule over you, or just one man? Remember, I am your flesh and blood.' (NIV)

The muddle of Gideon's family relationships bore poisonous fruit. Abimelek, the son of Gideon's concubine, thirsted after power. He incited his mother's relatives to rebellion and took for himself the high calling of kingship. To establish his position he slaughtered all the potential opposition except for Jotham, Gideon's youngest son, who managed to escape. This young man was the only one left to warn the citizens of Shechem and Abimelek of their folly.

Fables such as the one yelled out by Jotham were popular among eastern peoples at this time, and all would have clearly understood its message. When offered the kingship, the 'good' trees—olive, fig and vine—chose to continue using their gifts to serve others rather than to rule. Only the worthless bramble was presumptuous enough to aspire to such leadership—an image of Abimelech. The bramble causes harm to those who seek its shelter, as the rebels experienced.

When Jesus' disciples were arguing about who was the greatest among them, Jesus said, 'The greatest among you should be like the youngest, and the one who rules like the one who serves… I am among you as one who serves' (Luke 22:26–27). Our majestic King of kings and Lord of lords viewed his leadership role as a serving one, which he demonstrated so compellingly when he washed his disciples' grimy feet.

We regularly see people grasping for power on our world stage, but it is equally damaging in smaller environments. A bully is never pleasant, whether at home, school, work or play, but especially at church. Whatever leadership role we are granted, let's make sure we are following Jesus and being servant leaders.

My servant king, would you give me the leadership roles you want me to have, so I can use the gifts you've given me. Help me to be an example of a servant leader to all those around me.

CHRISTINE PLATT

Whom do you worship?

After [the Shechemites] had gone out into the fields and gathered the grapes and trodden them, they held a festival in the temple of their god. While they were eating and drinking, they cursed Abimelek. (NIV)

Bringing in the grape harvest should have been a joyous occasion when the people gave thanks to God for blessing the fruit of the vine. Not so on this occasion. The people ignored God and feasted in a pagan temple. The celebration soon degenerated into cursing and threats of rebellion. Thus they unleashed violence against themselves and ultimately all were murdered.

It could have been so different. The people of Shechem repeatedly changed their allegiance and it all went downhill—from Gideon's sons, to Abimelek, then to Gaal. It seems that no one thought of recalling Gideon's example of faith and turning back to God. They should also have known of Abraham, Sarah, Moses and Joseph, whose lives illustrated God's continual rescue and provision for his people in the past. But they chose to worship a pagan god and thank it for the harvest. Why?

It does seem easier to follow a leader you can see, rather than one you have to trust in by faith, and it does take courage to stand against the majority mob rule. But the consequences of forgetting God are dire, as the inhabitants of Shechem experienced.

In Romans 15:4 we read, 'For everything that was written in the past was written to teach us, so that through the endurance taught in the Scriptures and the encouragement they provide we might have hope.' By reading of God's dealings with humanity over the centuries, we learn to recognise godly examples to follow and other examples to avoid. If you'd been there in Shechem, what would you have done? Would you have joined your friends and neighbours in the pagan temple or would you have been brave enough to buck the trend and worship the one true God?

Consider your response to this question and relate it to your everyday life. Do you just go with the flow or are you prepared to stand up for what is right and good and true?

CHRISTINE PLATT

Humility versus pride

Abimelek went to the tower and attacked it... A woman dropped an upper millstone on his head and cracked his skull. Hurriedly he called to his armour-bearer, 'Draw your sword and kill me, so that they can't say, "A woman killed him."' (NIV)

Abimelek's pride was hurt when the people of Shechem turned against him. He went on a rampage of murder and destruction, not only in Shechem but also in another town, Thebez. But he got too close to the wall of the tower. Did he begin to think he was invincible?

In warfare at that time, while the men fought with bows, arrows and spears, the women dropped heavy stones from a high place on to the invaders below. Abimelek knew this strategy but was unaware that death was staring him in the face. The stone fell—a dead hit.

Even in his final moments, his pride surged to the fore. All he could think about was how he would be remembered and the disgrace of being killed by a woman. His strategy didn't work, though, because that's exactly how he was remembered (2 Samuel 11:21). The woman hurling the stone was the cause of his death, but it was his own pride that paved the way for his destruction. 'First pride—then the crash—the bigger the ego, the harder the fall' (Proverbs 16:18, *The Message*).

As we wrap up our readings, let's remember Gideon's humble attitude before God in the victory that God wrought over Midian. In contrast, Abimelek's pride brought horror and death to many and eventually to himself. God's word tells us, 'The Lord detests all the proud of heart. Be sure of this: they will not go unpunished' (Proverbs 16:5). Jesus, who of all people could be considered as having the right to be proud, resisted that temptation and was 'humble in heart' (Matthew 11:29).

With Jesus, Gideon and Abimelek in mind, reflect on Micah 6:8: 'The Lord has told you what is good, and this is what he requires of you: to do what is right, to love mercy, and to walk humbly with your God' (NLT).

CHRISTINE PLATT

Journeying in faith

Alison Teale writes…

I have found that we reach a stage of life when we realise we have come a very long way since our youth. Times have changed, people and things around us have changed, and we ourselves have changed—but, as we sit quietly at our metaphorical vantage point and look back at the path we have trodden, one thing a believer can say is that they have journeyed all that way in faith. Whether our faith has been strong or merely flickering, faith has moulded the journey and the journey has moulded our faith.

Through my journey of faith, I can quite happily say that I am not the person I used to be, but I am more myself in who I have become. Also, I *like* who I am, despite knowing that I still have a way to go. I am comfortable with myself, comfortable with my faith and comfortable with God. This does not mean that I have become a person who avoids challenges or lacks self-discipline, but that I approach these things more maturely, having tasted God's faithfulness in many testing life experiences over the last four decades since personal faith became a conscious reality in my life.

Perhaps entering midlife and having weathered various storms makes a person more reflective. One thing it does is to knock the rough edges off your character, in the same way that the constant pounding of waves rubs a stone into a smooth pebble. Over the next couple of weeks I want to share some of the lessons I have learned as part of my journeying in faith. I hope that they might be able to bring some encouragement to you, for although we all live different lives in different circumstances, under that veneer our stories have many similarities.

Above all, enjoy the journey. The journey is all we have, this side of heaven, and it is over all too soon. We need to be mindful of how blessed we are to experience the journey, whether the path is easy or steep, enjoying each step of the way. For as great as the promises awaiting us at the end may be, the journey is all we have in the present, so let's be able to say that we journeyed well.

Faith is the task of a lifetime

So I went down to the potter's house, and I saw him working at the wheel. But the pot he was shaping from the clay was marred in his hands; so the potter formed it into another pot, shaping it as seemed best to him. (NIV)

Social media is good for something. A few months ago I came across a post that talked about faith being 'the task of a lifetime'. As I was contemplating on life as a process of journeying in faith, I was immediately captivated by this thought. The article referred to in the post was a discussion of Søren Kierkegaard's concept of faith. To be honest, I did not have the energy to delve deeply into this Danish philosopher-theologian's thinking right at that moment, but the phrase 'faith is the task of a lifetime' struck a chord deep in my inner being and I did read the article.

I was living through a period of time after leaving a church that had cared for and supported me through a very difficult few years of my life, but I knew deep down that God was calling me on to something new. The decision to leave that congregation and go back to my Anglican roots was tumultuous and difficult. At moments I felt as if I was choosing to abandon my faith completely, but now I can see that this major turning point was crucial to the next phase of my walk with God. It was the prelude to a time of rest that I was glad to grab with both hands (Isaiah 30:15a). Rather like the clay in today's reading, I was mushed down from the shape in which I then found myself and gently remade in a rather different one, albeit from the same clay.

Initially it was strange to find myself in this new form, but I began to appreciate what God was doing in me. I realised that I was still walking hand in hand with him and my faith had taken a significant step forward.

Lord, when I find myself in unfamiliar territory, help me to realise that I have not left you behind me, but you are right beside me in the next step of the task of a lifetime.

ALISON TEALE

In the beginning

Therefore, if anyone is in Christ, the new creation has come: the old has gone, the new is here! All this is from God, who reconciled us to himself through Christ. (NIV)

Every journey has a beginning—not necessarily the moment we step out of the door, ticket in hand, but much further back when some deep desire moved us to make the decision to go. The reasons that prompted that decision may have been many. Perhaps we needed a rest or a change of scene; we may have wanted to visit a friend or relative, to do business or even to make a pilgrimage.

Journeying in faith is no different: it has a beginning. For many Christians, the beginning of this journey is marked by a moment of conversion or personal commitment, so that there is a distinct 'before' and 'after'. That moment, for me, was in the dormitory of a girls' boarding school one Sunday afternoon in 1972. I was eleven years old, on my own for the first time in my life. As I had arrived three weeks after the start of term, I was with strangers who had already formed friendships that would last the duration of their seven years' schooling, leaving me feeling always like the one tagging along. So when I asked Jesus into my heart, in as much privacy as can be found, sitting on a bed in a room that sleeps eight, it was not because I was convicted of any sins, but because I wanted Jesus to be my friend.

Thus started a journey that has now lasted well over 40 years and has taken me to some strange and wonderful places, both in my inner life and in the world at large. Older and wiser, I now realise that my journeying in faith started the moment I took my first breath. For us there may be a 'before' and 'after', but the Lord has been watching over each of us every step of the way.

Take time to recall any 'before' and 'after' moments you have experienced. Maybe describe them on paper. Looking back, can you now see God at work in your life even before that time?

ALISON TEALE

Remember, remember

Remember the wonders he has done, his miracles, and the judgements he pronounced. (NIV)

This week I have been describing for a friend a very long journey that I took as a child, when I lived with my family in southern Africa. I had made a scrapbook of the journey, but I discarded it rather rashly when I downsized some years ago, so taking time to remember the 4000-mile road trip to the coast and back was an enjoyable exercise that left me strangely energised and in touch with a younger self.

Taking time to stop and review our spiritual journey can have the same effect. We forget how far we have come and the incredible things we have seen and experienced along the way until we actively recall and review what has gone before. The act of remembering is an important part of the way we form our identity as individuals, as families and communities and even as nations. We are constantly adjusting our understanding of our current reality by examining and rearranging the pieces of our past. Remembering also gives us the opportunity to take another look at lessons learned and a chance to be grateful.

One aid to this task of remembering is to take a piece of A4 paper, fold it in half three times and then flatten it out so that it is divided neatly into eight sections. Take a pen or pencil and draw a simple image in each of the first seven sections, of key moments in your spiritual journey. If there is a Bible verse that was important to you in any of those moments, add it in. Spend some time thanking God for the distance he has brought you. Then prayerfully wait on God. What is he saying to you about the future? Draw your impressions in the eighth section and turn the exercise into further prayer.

Who am I, Sovereign Lord, and what is my family, that you have brought me this far?... Sovereign Lord, you have also spoken about the future' (2 Samuel 7:18–19).

ALISON TEALE

Life laundry

Therefore, since we are surrounded by such a great cloud of witnesses, let us throw off everything that hinders and the sin that so easily entangles. And let us run with perseverance the race marked out for us. (NIV)

My closest friend is about to emigrate to join her daughters and their families in Australia. Her journey began several years ago with the momentous decision to go. The preparation for emigrating has been a key part of the process. First she downsized from a large bungalow to a small flat, and now, a couple of years later, she is doing the final sorting of her possessions, ready for the international removal company to pack and ship them.

This activity has rubbed off on me. With my penchant for decluttering, I too have started another round of culling my possessions. I know in the back of my mind that a move may be in the offing for me, before too long, and that the place where I end up will probably be much smaller than where I currently live. Shedding possessions to make a radical move is not easy. Once the rubbish has been thrown away and the obvious junk has been donated, then begins the more complicated task of letting go of things we hold on to simply because they cost us a lot to acquire or they hold special memories. Then there are things we keep for aesthetic reasons or just because we think we might need them.

Sometimes our attachment to things holds us back; stuff needs to go because we can't take it with us on the next leg of the journey. The same is true of our inner lives. We haul around emotional and spiritual baggage that we simply need to put down, sort through, dispose of and leave behind. Yet it takes time to clear out the inner life, just as it does the external life. Don't be disheartened by the magnitude of the process. The key thing is to begin and then to persist.

Search me, God, and know my heart; test me and know my anxious thoughts. See if there is any offensive way in me, and lead me in the way everlasting (Psalm 139:23–24).

ALISON TEALE

The valley of tears

Therefore I am now going to allure her; I will lead her into the wilderness and speak tenderly to her. There I will give her back her vineyards, and will make the Valley of Achor a door of hope. (NIV)

During our lives we are bound to have challenging times. Christians sometimes express this by saying that we can't always live on the mountain top; sometimes we find ourselves down in the valley. We can easily roll ourselves into the metaphorical valley by losing our footing and doing something we regret. Getting back on our feet may be painful, mainly due to our pride and perhaps due to the condemnation of others, but God's grace helps us stand tall again if we come to him in repentance.

Yet there are times when something happens to us, and nothing we have done or not done seems to have caused the valley in which we find ourselves. For me, one such valley was several years of postnatal depression, and another was a time when I was grieving more deeply than I realised over my father's death. For others, it could mean coming to terms with a major illness, redundancy or unexpected accident. These are all times in which we experience the 'valley of tears'.

The Valley of Achor (which means 'trouble') was a place where a whole family was stoned to death due to one man's dishonesty (Joshua 7), but today's passage from Hosea contains wonderful promises in which God says that he will make a door of hope in the dark places in which we find ourselves. In my first valley, I searched frantically for the door of hope as if it was a magical portal that would allow me to exit immediately. Now I am old enough to know that the door is a matter of having faith and persevering in the day-to-day until the adverse time passes and we find ourselves on the other side of it, strengthened and ready for what life holds next.

He lifted me out of the slimy pit, out of the mud and mire; he set my feet on a rock and gave me a firm place to stand (Psalm 40:2).

ALISON TEALE

Straight paths

Trust in the Lord with all your heart and lean not on your own understanding; in all your ways submit to him, and he will make your paths straight. Do not be wise in your own eyes; fear the Lord and shun evil. (NIV)

A friend gave me today's verse when we were still young enough to fit into the awful green uniform that our school insisted we wear. I still have the postcard on which the verse is printed. It's rather dog-eared now and the design of the rose that adorns it is rather dated, but the verse itself is one that I have held on to through four decades, and it holds as true for me today as it did back then. Can I look back and say that the Lord has made my way straight? I think I can.

That doesn't mean the road has not gone up and down on numerous occasions, but, looking back, there does seem to have been coherence in the path I have trodden. Some of the things I have experienced are things I do not understand. Some things I have done, which seemed to be right at the time, appear to have been a waste of time, but I believe that nothing is wasted in the kingdom of God. It may be that the thing I currently consider 'wasted experience' will become invaluable in situations I am yet to face.

Other things have been unbearably painful—loss of many kinds. Yet even in these searingly difficult periods of life, the Lord has been faithful in what I have experienced. I have found my faith refined and I have been drawn closer to God in new ways while deepening my understanding of life itself. If we fear the Lord, let us live as he wants us to live, according to what we comprehend from his word. Let us 'keep hold of the deep truths of the faith with a clear conscience' (1 Timothy 3:9) so that our foothold may not be shaken.

The fear of the Lord is the beginning of wisdom; all who follow his precepts have good understanding. To him belongs eternal praise (Psalm 111:10).

ALISON TEALE

Settled at the crossroads

Terah took his son Abram, his grandson Lot son of Haran, and his daughter-in-law Sarai, the wife of his son Abram, and together they set out from Ur of the Chaldeans to go to Canaan. But when they came to Harran, they settled there. (NIV)

Abraham's journey from Ur to Canaan is a well-known story, but in fact it was Abraham's father Terah who made the decision to uproot the family and set out into the unknown, a decision based only on the promise that God had made to his son. After a while, the family came to Harran, a crossroads for various trading routes. Naturally they stopped there.

Many commentators make much of the fact that they stayed too long at the crossroads at Harran and draw the conclusion that Terah lacked faith and obedience to go further, thus preventing Abraham from moving on until he had died. This may be unfair: perhaps Terah wanted to continue but was too frail to travel further. Whatever the reason, though, the family was stuck there until Terah died.

We too have times in our lives when we are stuck at a metaphorical crossroads. It is not that we don't know which way to go or that we do not have the courage or faith to make a decision, but rather because those for whom we have responsibility are preventing us from doing anything other than remaining stationary for a while.

In Jewish culture, it was assumed that people would care for elderly relatives, so Abram could not move on until he had discharged his duty. We also may have to wait until we have discharged duties to our families before we can go where we believe God is calling us. Trust is the key. I have found that waiting is all part of God's greater plan and there is much we can learn while we are waiting to move on.

Lord, when it seems that we are stuck at a junction in life, give us faith to know you are with us in the waiting, teaching us lessons for the journey ahead.

ALISON TEALE

When you don't know what to do

Nathan replied to the king, 'Whatever you have in mind, go ahead and do it, for the Lord is with you.' (NIV)

There have been times in my life when I've found myself so overwhelmed by a situation that I've not known what to do. These were not 'crossroad' situations where I had the luxury of waiting on the Lord for direction or needed a prod to get up and get moving. They were the sort of overwhelming challenges in which it can be difficult to still our inner being for long enough to hear what the Lord might be saying.

What do we do when we don't know what to do? In my experience, we need to draw on the spiritual reserves we have laid down in easier times. If we are walking with God according to his word, and his character is being formed in us by his Holy Spirit, then I believe we will instinctively know what to do in the short term, even if we are very unsure how things will turn out in the long run. Just as we need to forget what lies behind as we move forward on our journey, sometimes we need not concern ourselves too much about what lies ahead, but must just do what is obviously the next right thing at a given moment.

As we walk obediently step by step, each subsequent decision will become clear. Some steps are harder and cost us more dearly than others, but we are not walking into unknown territory on our own. We have our hand in the hand of someone who cares for us deeply and fiercely. So learn to trust your spiritually honed instincts. Having a friend or mentor to check in with is also invaluable, but eventually we have to be decisive and take the next small step in the right direction.

Thank you, Lord, that when I am walking hand in hand with you I can step out in confidence, knowing that you are there to guide, steady and reassure me.

ALISON TEALE

Travelling companions

I hope to see you while passing through and to have you assist me on my journey there, after I have enjoyed your company for a while... so that I may come to you with joy, by God's will, and in your company be refreshed. (NIV)

Through the three decades of my marriage, I did not have any really close friends or a mentor. I knew a lot of people, because the man who was my husband was in full-time ministry and had a significant position of leadership, but I had no one outside the immediate family with whom I was particularly close.

During the few years I have been on my own, I have learned to appreciate the handful of women who committed themselves to be there for me, once I found myself alone. Learning to have real friends and to be a real friend has been an exhilarating experience. Two women in particular were just there to listen, faithfully, week by week, and sometimes at the drop of a hat when I needed extra support. There were those who gave me financial support or delivered bags of groceries, and those who invited me out for a meal or to an event so that I wasn't stuck in the house evening after evening or weekend after weekend. Others texted or emailed me messages of encouragement or phoned me when my presence was missed.

These wonderful people have helped me on my way and I would not be where I am without them. Besides the help, I have learned simply to enjoy their company. As time has passed and my wounds have healed, I have had the immense joy of becoming able to reciprocate their generosity, learning to give back with a genuine heart, learning to listen to them the way they have listened to me and being able to give sacrificially of my time and energy when they have been ill and in need of someone to be there for them. Friends are refreshing—and the question is, 'Are we refreshing to our friends'?

Thank you, Lord, for the travelling companions you have put in my path, for the unexpected joy of being able to share life with good friends.

ALISON TEALE

Significant others

Now we ask you, brothers and sisters, to acknowledge those who work hard among you, who care for you in the Lord and who admonish you. Hold them in the highest regard in love because of their work. (NIV)

Each of our lives is marked by the people who have played a significant part in making us who we are today. Taking time to think back over these people and the impact they have had on our lives is a useful practice. Not only does it give us an opportunity for gratitude, and to pray for them if they are still alive, but it brings us a renewed sense of appreciation of the person we have become by the intervention of God in our lives through them.

One key person in my life was the mistress of the boarding house where I lived when I was sent away to school at the age of eleven. The weekly compulsory chapel meetings that she led on a Sunday afternoon were instrumental in my coming to faith, and I have kept in touch with her over the 40 or more years since that time. There were others, like the parents of my schoolfriend who took me into their home when my mother was hospitalised, or the woman who turned up on my doorstep one day, befriended me and looked after the babies on a regular basis so that I could have much-needed time to myself.

A while back, I wrote to one particular woman, since deceased, and thanked her for making a decision that changed the course of my life for the better. Taking time to thank those who have influenced our lives for good is an important discipline, an act of kindness and appreciation. It not only returns the blessing and encouragement we have been so freely given; it also blesses and encourages us in return. Why not think about who has influenced your life and thank them while there is still time.

Lord, may I never be so lax as to withhold an act of gratitude from one who obviously deserves it, for the input they have made into my life.

ALISON TEALE

Sacred places

When Jacob awoke from his sleep, he thought, 'Surely the Lord is in this place, and I was not aware of it.' (NIV)

Are there places that have had or still have a special meaning for you? Places where you had a deep encounter with God and remain landmark spots for you, or places that have meant a lot to you over a longer period of your spiritual formation? In today's reading we meet Jacob, who fell asleep, funnily enough, on the way to Harran—the crossroads I mentioned before. In his sleep, Jacob had a dream in which the Lord reaffirmed to him the promises he had made to Jacob's ancestor Abraham—and Jacob had a vision of the angels ascending and descending a ladder into heaven.

One place that holds special significance for me is the derelict walled kitchen garden of a retreat house where I sat in silence and contemplated what the Lord had in store for me next. My eyes caught sight of a Spirea bush, covered in a profusion of white blossom. This bush is commonly known as 'bridal wreath'. As I sat in the sunshine, drinking in its extravagant simplicity, some verses from Song of Solomon came to my mind: 'Arise, my love, my fair one, and come away; for now the winter is past, the rain is over and gone. The flowers appear upon the earth; the time of singing has come' (2:10–12, NRSV).

I felt I was being encouraged that a new season was coming in my life, in which I would do fulfilling things, and indeed that proved to be the case. On a more current basis, one of my sacred spaces is the local nature reserve where I can walk with my dogs at the weekend and sit enjoying a moment of solitude. God may be everywhere, but there are places where he seems closer to us. Where are your sacred places?

Thank you, Lord, for the places where we can draw aside, still our hearts and know that we will meet you—the places where, for us, heaven and earth meet.

ALISON TEALE

The God of surprises

However, as it is written: 'What no eye has seen, what no ear has heard, and what no human mind has conceived—the things God has prepared for those who love him.' (NIV)

I recently took a trip to the cinema on my own for the very first time. In the past I have always had a friend or family member with me. I went to watch the sequel to a film about the adventures of a group of pensioners who have made their home in India. The original movie had entranced me and I wanted to see what the characters did next.

One of the main characters is a grumpy but good-hearted spinster who has been ungratefully cast off by the family who employed her as a nanny for many years. She has travelled to India reluctantly, to get a cheap hip replacement operation after a fall. When events conspire to force her out of her self-pity and prejudice, she takes on the job of managing the hotel where she is staying, making it into a resounding success.

At the end of the second film, this character gives a monologue, reflecting on the past and wondering with incredulity at how she has found herself, at the end of her life, managing a hotel on the other side of the world. It was the last thing she expected.

The film is not religious in nature, but each character is on a spiritual journey, a journey of self-discovery, in just the same way as you or I. For this character, a fall and a broken hip take her to places she would never have considered otherwise.

I constantly stand amazed at the good and surprising things that God allows to spring out of what seems immediately bad, making all things new. Today's verse may be talking about the life to come, but I very much believe that God is also a God of surprises in the here and now. Are you ready for what he might bring?

'May the God of Surprises delight you, inviting you to accept gifts not yet imagined' (Elizabeth Eiland Figueroa: www.ignatianspirituality.com)

ALISON TEALE

I know who holds the future

Even to your old age and grey hairs I am he, I am he who will sustain you. I have made you and I will carry you; I will sustain you and I will rescue you. (NIV)

Last week I mentioned people who have played a significant part in my life. Recently I lost one of those people, as did many others whom this amazing woman of God had touched. I did not know her well, but she was always there to welcome me into church, whether she was on hospitality duty or not. Her embrace and smile helped me feel valued at a time when it would have been easy to feel condemned and to have vanished into myself.

Apart from the very obvious lesson she taught us all about how valuable even the smallest gesture of kindness can be to a hurting soul, this woman was a living demonstration of how to live bountifully in old age. She lived in a mobile home, she dressed simply, gave freely of her time and resources to many charities, religious and secular, and I often met her at 'food-tasting' sessions where we had both turned up to earn an extra few pounds by tasting new products for a marketing company. She was living the abundant life that Jesus promised his followers: her mind was firmly fixed on things above, she was seeking the kingdom of God and 'all things had been added to her', just as Jesus had promised.

Being on the threshold of old age, I found it a valuable experience to take time to go to her memorial service and contemplate whether I would journey as well in my final years as she had clearly done. It made me think that if we were to write our own eulogy, how would it read? How would we like it to read? What changes would we need to make to close any gap between the two versions?

Thank you, Lord, that you are there to sustain us as we journey through old age, so that we can be as useful to you in those years as in the years that have gone before.

ALISON TEALE

Run with it

I will stand at my watch and station myself on the ramparts; I will look to see what he will say to me... Then the Lord replied: 'Write down the revelation and make it plain on tablets so that a herald may run with it.' (NIV)

In this final note on journeying in faith, I would like to advocate the practice of journalling. I began about three years ago and it has proved very beneficial. Research in the psychological sciences has shown that people who keep a journal are emotionally (and, I'd like to think, spiritually) healthier than those who do not. Apparently the act of committing what is bothering us to paper has a purgative effect on the mind and reduces stress levels. Writing down why a person means so much to us is also good for our inner well-being, as is recording a list of three things we can be grateful for each day.

Although my journal does contain a record of what I think God is saying to me at any one time and how I am going to respond to him, it also contains a brutally honest record of my secret heart, bursts of appreciation for those who have had an impact on my life, and lists of all the good things I have to be thankful for.

When times have been hard, I have made a discipline of writing every day; when times have been easier, I have spent much longer on my journal, but only on a weekly or twice-weekly basis. Besides the cumulative effect of these writing practices, a journal helps you look back and remember how far you have journeyed. Sometimes I sit and read what I wrote a year ago and I always marvel at how running with what I have made plain on paper has changed me in the intervening months.

So my parting challenge to you would be to start a journal, be honest with yourself and God—and run with it.

Lord, we stop and thank you again for your faithfulness, for bringing us this far and for all that you have taught us along the way. We ask that you will help us run with what you have prepared for our future.

ALISON TEALE

Colossians: Jesus, be the centre

Jennifer Rees Larcombe writes…

'I believe in God, but I don't do Jesus. Surely he was just one of those gurus?' I was beginning to write these notes when I overheard that remark in a checkout queue and realised, 'That's the kind of thinking that prompted Paul to write his letter to Colosse.'

Chained in a Roman prison, he had been delighted to hear how well the church there had been going (Colossians 1:3–5) since being planted by his friend Epaphras. Colosse was a prosperous town in western Turkey: the townsmen raised sheep in fertile pastureland, dyed the wool and exported cloth all over the Roman empire.

The church expanded enthusiastically until it began to be infiltrated by a group of intellectuals called Gnostics, whose philosophical ideas and academic debates were subtly undermining the central position of Jesus and the cross (Colossians 2:8). Paul's letter was written to encourage the believers to keep Jesus as the centre of their lives.

Tragically, all through the centuries, churches and individual Christians have continued to allow other things to take his central place. Theological argument, power struggles, good works, religious ceremonies, greed and sin—all push Jesus out. Christianity would have died long ago if the Holy Spirit had not regularly brought 'times of refreshing… from the Lord' (Acts 3:19), leading us back to Jesus as our pivotal point once again.

If, on a piece of paper, you drew a big circle to represent your life, where would you draw a cross to denote Jesus? Is he being pushed out of the centre by activity, difficult emotions or something you love more than him? Over the coming week, why don't we all use this letter that Paul wrote about Jesus to consider his level of importance and place in our lives?

What is God like?

We look at this Son and see the God who cannot be seen... For everything, absolutely everything, above and below, visible and invisible... *everything* got started in him and finds its purpose in him. He was there before any of it came into existence and holds it all together right up to this moment. (*The Message*)

God had a problem. He longed for humans to understand how much he loved them. He wanted to be involved in the details of their lives—to help, comfort and guide them—but to most people he was an invisible spirit, distant, frightening and unreachable. He knew we could never understand his love unless we saw it in human eyes or human actions; we could not hear his voice unless it spoke in simple human words.

So God came, in the person of his Son Jesus, for two main reasons: to show us exactly what God is like (how he thinks, feels and acts) and to take on himself the death sentence that our sins deserved.

Whatever must it have been like for those twelve ordinary men, his first disciples, to live, eat and travel with God-in-disguise for three years? At first they probably thought he was just an exceptionally wonderful man. Gradually, though, they realised that everything they witnessed Jesus saying or doing was like another piece of a jigsaw puzzle being put into place until, eventually, it showed a glorious portrait of God himself. One of them later wrote, 'The infinite Life of God himself took shape before us' (1 John 1:2). Finally, Thomas, the last to be convinced, had to fall on his knees before Jesus and say, 'My Lord and my God' (John 20:28, NIV).

Paul, backed by the apostles' witness, wanted to assure the Colossians that Jesus was not simply a prophet sent to bring God's message, but God himself—in control of the universe. I love verse 17! It is wonderful to know that when everything seems to be disintegrating around us, Jesus actually has it all in hand. I just wish I would remember that more often.

Lord, I am sorry that my problems so often fill the centre of my life and push you out. I keep trying to work things out myself instead of trusting you to hold all the mess together for me.

JENNIFER REES LARCOMBE

The download

We also pray that you will be strengthened with all his glorious power so you will have all the endurance and patience you need. May you be filled with joy, always thanking the Father. (NLT)

To be honest, I'm not sure I would have wanted Paul to pray for me in the way he did for those church members in Colosse. Christians in other parts of the Roman empire were facing persecution for treason. Caesar was Rome's god, as well as its king, but Christians put Jesus in Caesar's place. While the Colossians were not yet facing torture and death, conversion to Christianity meant unpopularity and potential loss of livelihood.

If my life were that uncertain, I'd prefer Paul to pray for protection, prosperity and peace. Instead, though, he was asking for power to endure trouble (and difficult people) with patience and joy (v. 11).

I recently went to see a close friend in a hospice. She had lived such a happy life, she would often say, 'I'm not sure I'll cope if things ever go wrong.' There she was, though, with only days to live, wracked with pain and obvious concern for her husband and family, and her face was radiant. 'It's like you get this download from heaven of all the strength and joy you need,' she explained, as God's presence filled her room like thick, warm custard.

Paul, who was also under a death sentence, wanted the Colossians (and us) to know that, when the inevitable hard times hit, God has this special download for us, too. It isn't the gritted-teeth, flinty-eyed type of endurance and patience, because he also offers us joy, and it's the joy of the Lord that gives us strength (Nehemiah 8:10). That's even better news. This download isn't only available during times of crisis; it can be ours in the irritating, tiring, ordinary days, too.

Could you be brave enough to jot down the situation you find most difficult or fear most? Then add the words of Colossians 1:11 and claim God's promise for yourself.

JENNIFER REES LARCOMBE

God's mysterious secret

My goal is... that they may know the mystery of God, namely, Christ, in whom are hidden all the treasures of wisdom and knowledge... So then, just as you received Christ Jesus as Lord, continue to live your lives in him, rooted and built up in him. (NIV)

Gnostics were telling the new Colossian Christians that the way to God was a mysterious secret process, known only to the educated intellectuals in their organisation (v. 8). Paul firmly tells them that God's 'mysterious secret' is Jesus himself (v. 2). 'You can stop striving and searching,' he says, 'because you already have him. Your relationship with him is real—organic, alive, growing and deepening. Your lives are joined to his life, so you must build everything you are and do on him and around him. You can find in him everything you will ever need in this life and the next.'

The same applies to us, too, and the more we realise the extent of what it means to be 'rooted' in Jesus (v. 7), the more of his life and strength we can draw from him.

Paul uses several wonderfully vivid ways of describing Jesus in order to counteract the vague, ethereal ideas of the Gnostics. I love the idea of Jesus likened to a chest full of hidden treasure (v. 3). The Passion translation of 1:27 gives us the same image: 'This Mystery of Christ embedded in us becomes a heavenly treasure chest of hope filled with the riches of glory for his people'.

I often hit situations in both my job and family where I suddenly find myself feeling discouraged and in need of hope or lacking the wisdom to know what to say or do next. I instinctively want to figure things out for myself and solve my own problems. However, I'm slowly learning that living my life in Christ means seeing Jesus as the source of all the hope and wisdom I need. All I have to do is reach into my treasure chest and pull out, by faith, whatever it is that I need.

Lord, I am sorry that sometimes my own independent thinking and self-confidence take the central place and I forget to build my life around you.

JENNIFER REES LARCOMBE

The power of the cross

For you were buried with Christ when you were baptised... You were dead because of your sins... Then God made you alive with Christ, for he forgave all our sins. He cancelled the record of the charges against us and took it away by nailing it to the cross. (NLT)

Many of the church members to whom Paul was writing would have been dramatically converted from the life of vice, abuse and immorality that pervaded many Roman communities. Through accepting the gospel, they would have been delighted to be rescued from the kingdom of darkness and transferred into Christ's kingdom of light (1:13). Then along came the Gnostics, undermining their faith in the cross by saying that to qualify for heaven you had to live a perfect life. Like the rest of us, they knew they continued to sin. Doubts about eternal life were beginning to spoil their joy.

Through my counselling, I meet a surprising number of Christians who don't understand the cross. They feel like second-class Christians because of something in the past that makes them feel ashamed. They may have asked God's forgiveness many times but they still secretly go on accusing themselves.

I often show them Paul's words (2:13–14) and get them to write down those accusations on pieces of paper. Then we take them down to the cross at the bottom of my garden, nail them up and put a match to them. The ashes blow away in the breeze.

Perhaps most of us find it easier to believe that the power of the cross can wipe away any major sin but we still feel shame over our secret habits, the kinds of things we certainly wouldn't want our church friends to know about. As we ask God's forgiveness yet again, we begin to wonder when his patience will run out. The glorious fact that Paul wanted the Colossians, and us, to grasp is this: Jesus also wants us to use the power of his cross to deal with those little besetting sins, perhaps not all at once, but gradually over time.

Lord, sometimes it is my sense of shame and defeat that fills me instead of the joy of knowing you. Help me remember that on the cross you gained victory over every power that tries to bring me down.

JENNIFER REES LARCOMBE

Living the new life

Set your hearts on things above, where Christ is, seated at the right hand of God... For you died, and your life is now hidden with Christ in God. When Christ, who is your life, appears, then you also will appear with him in glory. (NIV)

Colossian Christians would all have been baptised as an outward symbol of their inner conversion to Christ. Going under the water represented dying to their old sinful lives; coming up out of the water was like rising again as a completely new person. Such radical change takes time to implement, so Paul reminds them that many of the ways they used to think, feel and act are now dead.

Paul obviously isn't suggesting that Christians should exist in a holy bubble, disconnected from their local communities, friends and family. He makes that quite clear in tomorrow's reading. He means that when we begin to live in Christ, we 'die' to the attitudes, values, motivations and standards of the world.

For instance, we put giving above getting, helping above controlling, and forgiving above revenge. We stop thinking, 'I've only got this one life, so I'm entitled to happiness, a job, housing and good health care.' Jesus came to offer us infinitely more than just this life. So, rather than demanding that other people meet our needs, perhaps we could use our brief lives to care for others (Luke 9:23–25).

We are no longer earthbound, trapped under our circumstances. 'Don't shuffle along, eyes to the ground, absorbed with the things right in front of you,' says Paul (3:2, *The Message*). Because you exist inside Jesus, where he is you are, too. He's enthroned in the glorious heights of heaven, so you live way up above the circumstances, seeing life on earth from God's perspective.

Colossians 3:3 comforts me when I'm misunderstood and criticised for being a Christian. The word translated 'hidden' originally meant 'secretly stashed away'. Because we are so precious to him, God has hidden our real, inner self safely inside himself and Jesus.

It is not always bad things that crowd Jesus out. It can be good things that have become too important—sport, hobbies, Facebook, work or a friendship. Is Jesus 'your life' or has something else has taken his place?

JENNIFER REES LARCOMBE

Getting dressed

You have stripped off your old sinful nature... Put on your new nature... Clothe yourselves with tenderhearted mercy, kindness, humility, gentleness, and patience. Make allowance for each other's faults, and forgive anyone who offends you... Above all, clothe yourselves with love, which binds us all together in perfect harmony. (NLT)

Colosse lay in a valley by the River Lycus and, when its citizens became Christians, it was probably there that they were baptised. Before they plunged into the water, they took off their colourful robes to show that they were leaving behind their old lives (vv. 5–9) and afterwards they put on simple white clothes to symbolise their new lives as Christians (v. 10). Paul loved this 'taking off and putting on' image (see Romans 13:12–14), often urging Christians to 'put on Jesus' and wear his characteristics as if they were clothing.

Fiona worked in a busy office under a tyrannical line manager, whom she hated. The feeling was mutual and they both made each other's lives a misery. Then Fiona met Jesus and, when she discovered today's passage, she realised that things at work had to change. Patience, which means the power to endure whatever comes with a good attitude, was not one of Fiona's natural gifts, so she pictured herself 'putting it on' each morning as she got dressed.

At first, Trudy, the manager, seemed even worse. Then one day she said, 'Fiona, you're different! Why?' Fiona's reply, 'I've started going to church', was met with a scornful sniff, but soon their relationship had improved so much that Fiona took Trudy to an Alpha course.

Paul says that love is the most important article of clothing we need to put on each morning (v. 14). Like a large warm overcoat, it holds everything else together. The final item on Paul's list of clothing is peace (v. 15): perhaps he was thinking of a hat to crown the outfit. The evening when Trudy gave her testimony at church, she said, 'Suddenly peace reigned in our office; it just had to be supernatural.'

Lord, I so often forget that, whatever I do or say, I'm your representative. Help me to 'wear you' as I dash through my day.

JENNIFER REES LARCOMBE

Practise what you preach

Tychicus... is a dear brother, a faithful minister and fellow servant in the Lord... He is coming with Onesimus, our faithful and dear brother, who is one of you... My fellow prisoner Aristarchus sends you his greetings, as does Mark, the cousin of Barnabas... If he comes to you, welcome him. (NIV)

Two fascinating stories lie behind this list of greetings. Onesimus was a runaway slave belonging to a wealthy Colossian church member called Philemon. After his escape, Onesimus received Christ and he and Paul became friends. By describing this former slave as a 'dear brother', Paul was illustrating that in Christ we are all equal (3:11). Sadly, today we still value some Christians more highly than others. In a separate letter he urges Philemon to welcome his slave home and treat him as family. That was radical, outrageous forgiveness, at a time when slaves were often beaten to death for running away.

I once wrote a book on forgiveness. Years later, when my husband left me for another woman, I realised that it is far easier to urge others to forgive than to do it yourself. So was forgiving easy for Paul? The second story behind the list shows us that it was not. When he and Barnabas set out to evangelise the world, they took Mark, Barnabas' young relative, to help. Tragically, Mark let them down badly (Acts 13:13). Later, when Barnabas urged Paul to forgive Mark and take him on their next trip, Paul vehemently refused (15:37–39).

Paul obviously had a huge capacity for love. However, the more we love, the more rejection hurts—and the more difficult forgiveness becomes. Yet at some point God must have reminded Paul of his need to forgive and restore his relationship with Mark, so he made contact and eventually they even worked together again (2 Timothy 4:11). I love the way Paul urges the Colossians to welcome Mark—a definite fruit of forgiveness.

One of the main reasons why Jesus is pushed off-centre is our failure to forgive. Buried unforgiveness is deadly.

Ask Jesus to show you any broken friendships or people he wants you to contact again.

JENNIFER REES LARCOMBE

Acts 8—28: adventures in God

Tracy Williamson writes…

Helen Keller stated that 'life is either a daring adventure or nothing'. As someone who was both blind and deaf, she could easily have been negative, but she was filled with expectation for what each day would hold. She lived with adventure in her heart. This was so important to her that the alternative was 'nothing'. But how many of us today live in 'nothing' because we've put adventure behind us with our childhood toys?

The word 'adventure' may make us imagine others undertaking exciting sports or pursuing their passions into exotic or dangerous countries—gifted individuals who know what they want from life and go for it. However, we don't generally think of our own Christian lives as coming into the category of 'adventure'.

When I was asked to write on 'Adventures in God, based on Acts 8—28', I was pleased. There is nothing greater than the adventure of knowing God and being trusted by him to be part of all he is doing. The book of Acts is full of exciting stories about ordinary people who made themselves available to God and were ready to embark on the adventure of following the Holy Spirit wherever he led. These people believed that even in the midst of everyday activities God wants to speak to us and use us as channels of his love.

Seeing how the early disciples manifested God's power, do we feel intimidated and distance ourselves, thinking that he won't work like that through us? Paul prays in Ephesians 1:19 that we will know 'his incomparably great power for us who believe'. Believing is the key to using that power; it is for us all.

Over the next fortnight we will discover what the stories in Acts reveal of God's amazing character. We may find ourselves challenged to take a step; we may start to hear him; we may experience his comfort, joy or healing as we embark on the adventure of living in his love and forgiveness and giving it away to others.

Carrying his presence

Saul began to destroy the church. Going from house to house, he dragged off both men and women and put them in prison. Those who had been scattered preached the word wherever they went. (NIV)

Acts 8 starts with a tragedy. Stephen has just been stoned to death, and a 'great persecution broke out against the church in Jerusalem, and all except the apostles were scattered'.

Think for a moment of all that was going on. The disciples' beloved Lord Jesus had been crucified; then they had experienced the incredible joy of his resurrection and the coming of the Holy Spirit. Then, in the midst of the glory of seeing God working in awesome ways, one of their number was martyred and persecution swept Jerusalem. They had to flee the city that was their home. There was no time to gather their possessions or take care of dependants. They just had to run for their lives, to wherever their feet took them. There is no doubt that they would have been overwhelmed, confused and terrified, both for themselves and for their loved ones. Yet what the Bible focuses on is that they 'preached the word wherever they went'.

I find this amazingly encouraging. Most of us won't ever experience this level of persecution but we do all experience overwhelming or traumatic events in our lives. How do we react? I get 'thrown' by completely mundane but unexpected occurrences. I panic, thinking I can't cope, and sometimes my reactions don't reflect at all that Jesus is in my life.

He wants to work through us in every situation, just as he did with these disciples. They carried his presence in their hearts; they listened to his voice and received his strength, comfort and guidance. They refused to speak out thoughts of fear, rather speaking powerfully about Jesus to all they met. Because they focused on the reality of his presence more than their dread of suffering, they lived these circumstances as an adventure in God and not a paralysing trauma.

Lord Jesus, please help me to live life as an adventure, whatever the circumstances. Thank you that I carry your powerful presence in my heart and you want to use me to touch those around me with your love.

TRACY WILLIAMSON

Transforming lives

When they believed Philip as he proclaimed the good news… they were baptised, both men and women. Simon himself believed and was baptised. And he followed Philip everywhere, astonished by the great signs and miracles he saw. (NIV)

Do we recognise the incredible potential we have to transform people's lives? Philip was just an ordinary disciple like us, but he was passionate for God. When Philip fled to Samaria, he immediately started 'proclaiming the Christ'. As he shared, God worked powerfully, bringing multiple healings and deliverance. Then we see the impact on an individual—the sorcerer Simon. From being someone who amazed people with his own evil powers, he now acknowledges the far greater power of the Holy Spirit, is saved and baptised.

I feel very challenged by this. I can be quite fearful of those who practise occult or other faiths. I remember the time when a Jehovah's Witness knocked on my door and all I could think of was how quickly I could get rid of him. I was fearful of being negatively affected by his beliefs.

How often do we attribute greater power to the enemy than to the God who is Lord over all and who lives within us? The fact is, as this story shows, that people are hungry for the truth of God, whatever they currently believe or practise. What we have is greater than anything else because it is truly of God.

Sometimes I feel inadequate but, as this story shows, God wants us to be in the adventure of using our gifts together. Philip didn't have all the answers, even though he was doing miracles and was used to bring salvation to Simon. It was through Peter and John that the Samaritans received the Holy Spirit and it was Peter who had the wisdom to confront Simon about his wrong thinking. All three of them moved Simon further along in his journey of transformation. We are not alone but are linked together in the adventure of letting God work through us. The result is changed lives.

Will we trust in the one who is within us? 'We are joined to him; Satan is under our feet. We are seated on high and all authority is given to us through him' (from 'Jesus is Lord of all', © Marilyn Baker).

TRACY WILLIAMSON

Divine encounters

Now an angel of the Lord said to Philip, 'Go south...' So he started out, and on his way he met an Ethiopian eunuch, an important official in charge of all the treasury of the Kandake (which means 'queen of the Ethiopians'). (NIV)

This story reads like a Disney fantasy, but it reveals the reality of the spiritual realm and God's joy in making divine connections. What the angel instructed, Philip did. We may think we can't hear God like that, but God wants to communicate to us all and his timing is always perfect. All he wants is our trusting responsiveness to his voice.

I became a Christian when a fellow student sensed Father God asking her to tell me how much he loved me. Ruth didn't know that, just the week before, I'd tried to commit suicide, as I was in great emotional pain. I was desperate, but when I heard her sharing about God's love, something very deep inside me began to unlock and I became a Christian just three weeks later.

However they occur, divine encounters are always potentially life-changing and we need to be ready to respond to his prompting. For Ruth, it came as a heart-nudging to contact me. For Philip, it says that an angel spoke to him. We don't know exactly how that happened, but God had a plan, which he communicated step by step. Initially, all Philip knew was that he had to go south. This meant travelling on an unused desert road and it must have puzzled Philip, as he was in the midst of revival in Samaria. Why leave now? Still, he went, and God honoured his obedience. How often do we miss wonderful opportunities because we hold back when we don't understand everything?

Incredibly, Philip arrived just in time to hear the eunuch reading and questioning a passage in Isaiah. How else could Philip have connected with this man who was so culturally different? God's timing is amazing. The end result was joyful salvation and an open door for the gospel to reach Africa.

Thank God for all the occasions that you now realise were divine encounters. Ask his forgiveness for times you've sensed his prompting but held back out of fear. Choose to live in adventure.

TRACY WILLIAMSON

Stepping through our fears

Then Ananias went to the house and entered it. Placing his hands on Saul, he said, 'Brother Saul, the Lord—Jesus, who appeared to you on the road as you were coming here—has sent me so you may see again and be filled with the Holy Spirit.' (NIV)

I love this story and the deep insights it teaches us. Adventure is all about passion, believing in something with your whole being and acting accordingly. This was Saul's personality and, as a zealous Jew, he was on a divine mission to eradicate this heretical new church. The stakes were high and deadly serious. It challenges me to realise that we can become totally focused on a goal that is not from God. We may then be in a very dangerous position, affecting others as well as ourselves.

In contrast, Ananias is a fearful adventurer, even though his mission is undoubtedly God-ordained. He hears God clearly but is instantly thrown into panic: 'Lord… I have heard many reports about this man' (v. 13). I personally find this comforting, as I am the same. I easily panic and ask, 'Have I got this right?' or 'What if that happens?' The 'facts' we think we know can be daunting, so how do we react?

Sometimes we try to deny our fears and 'claim the victory'. Other times we listen more to the fear than to God and become paralysed. Ananias shows us a different way: he expressed those fears in dialogue with God, but still chose to listen and trust his word and be changed. We see how Ananias changes by the way he connects with Saul. He is no longer fearful but is filled with God's compassion. He touches Saul and calls him 'brother'. How wonderful that his fear has been so transformed!

We are all in the adventure of hearing God's call to communicate his love, but even more wonderful is the adventure of being changed deep inside so that our response to God springs out of a heart of compassion, not of fear.

'You are my hiding-place; you will protect me from trouble and surround me with songs of deliverance. I will instruct you and teach you in the way you should go; I will counsel you' (Psalm 32:7–8).

TRACY WILLIAMSON

Doing Christ's works

[Peter] took [Tabitha] by the hand and helped her to her feet. Then he called for the believers, especially the widows, and presented her to them alive. This became known all over Joppa, and many people believed in the Lord. (NIV)

This story of two amazing miracles, the healings of Aeneas and Tabitha, shows the powerful anointing that God has given us to do his works. It's not just about works, as wonderful as they are, but becoming Christ-like in our thoughts and ways. This happens for us as it did for Peter, by spending time with God, seeking to grow ever deeper in our understanding of him.

The way Peter ministered to Aeneas, even the very words he used about tidying his mat, were like a mirror image of the way Jesus had ministered. Peter's response to the news about Tabitha, the way he dealt with the grieving relatives, then prayed and helped her to stand, were all reflections of Jesus. Peter had lived with Jesus and watched him communicate with his Father, give individuals loving attention, pray for the sick and display God-given confidence in the face of impossible odds. All these things had a deep impact on Peter, but we have seen little evidence of that until now. During his years with Jesus, Peter, like many of us, vacillated between doubt, faith, fear and certainty. Ultimately the weaknesses triumphed in his disowning of Jesus.

Similarly, the weaknesses in our own lives can seem to triumph at times. I often fall into my old negative traits of feeling a failure—so much so that I withdraw from people or stop ministering in a certain way, believing I am inadequate. I then need to start listening to God again and taking in his truths.

It wasn't enough for Peter to physically be with Jesus. After the Holy Spirit came, Peter truly began to change. The key to such change is being filled with the Holy Spirit, communing with him, reflecting on his word and asking him to make us like Jesus.

'Sitting at his feet, that's where I long to be. Drawing close to him, more of his heart I see. Listening to his word, obeying what I've heard, opening my life to him in every part' (from 'Sitting at his feet' © Marilyn Baker).

TRACY WILLIAMSON

Seeing into heavenly realms (1)

One day at about three in the afternoon [the centurion] had a vision. He distinctly saw an angel of God who came to him and said, 'Cornelius!' (NIV)

As God's beloved children, we can enter heavenly realms through his gifts of knowledge, prophecy, vision or angelic messengers. They are inaccessible to our human senses alone, but God wants us all to experience them. As Joel 2:28 describes, 'I will pour out my Spirit on all people.' Today we are still in the period prophesied by Joel and described in Acts.

How do we step into this adventure? For Cornelius, who wasn't even a full believer, an angel came in a vision and spoke his name. It's important to reflect on this, as it gives us true and deep understanding of God's heart for us. He is our Father and Friend. He knows our names, and all that we are and all that we do matters to him. The angel told Cornelius, 'Your prayers and gifts to the poor have come up as a memorial offering before God' (10:4). How wonderful that God so affirmed him! The first time I heard God, I had only been a Christian a short time and was very depressed. I was walking from my college hostel through lovely countryside. I was too low to notice the scenery but suddenly had a strong feeling that I must stop and look. As I drank in the beauty, I heard a whisper in my heart: 'I made all this so that you can see what I am like, but none of this is as beautiful to me as you are.' I was stunned! I knew it had to be God because there was no way I could think such thoughts on my own.

Through the Holy Spirit, God opened my heart to hear his voice of love, affirming me and teaching me to hear him for others. You too can know this experience, and there is nothing more exciting.

Thank you, Father, that as your precious child I've been given your Holy Spirit, so that I can see into your heavenly realms. Please come and fill me, dear Lord. Open my ears to hear your voice and my eyes to see.

TRACY WILLIAMSON

Seeing into heavenly realms (2)

[Peter] became hungry and wanted something to eat, and while the meal was being prepared, he fell into a trance. He saw heaven opened and something like a large sheet being let down to earth… It contained all kinds of four-footed animals, as well as reptiles and birds. Then a voice told him, 'Get up, Peter. Kill and eat.' (NIV)

We now discover how experiencing the heavenly realm always changes us. Jesus had told the disciples many times to preach the good news to the Gentiles as well as the Jews, but they were too entrenched in their old beliefs to hear. Peter needed this vision from the Holy Spirit to understand God's plan.

How do such visions come to us? An important clue is found in verse 9: 'About noon the following day… Peter went up on the roof to pray.' Peter felt compelled to pray. I often feel this compulsion but don't necessarily follow it up. The story reveals how important it is to follow divine nudges when they come to us, not hours or days later. At the very time he was praying, God was drawing Cornelius' men to his house. God is working through our prayers even when we don't realise it.

The next clue is that it was lunch time and Peter was hungry (v. 10). This is significant, revealing how God takes ordinary things to heavenly heights in order to speak to us. Peter's thoughts were on food; thus the vision was about food.

Our life experiences, creation and ordinary things are all channels for his voice. If something draws our attention or an idea fills our mind, it can indicate that God wants to speak to us about it. Then we can ask, 'Lord, what do you want to say to me through this?' We may be amazed at the powerful outcome: in Peter's case, an entire Gentile family became Christians.

Lord, thank you for your Holy Spirit. Please help me go deeper into the adventure of hearing your voice and seeing into the heavenly realm so that I can truly be part of all you are doing.

TRACY WILLIAMSON

Being in God's plan

The church in Jerusalem... sent Barnabas to Antioch to investigate. He arrived and saw God's grace in action there, so he rejoiced and urged them to remain faithful to the Lord, to maintain an enduring, unshakeable devotion... A very large number of people were brought to the Lord. (The Voice)

The joy of being in the centre of what God is doing is like no other. I once visited Niagara Falls but first saw it from a distance. From there it looked like a typical river scene, but closer it was exhilarating. This was no languid stream but was roaring powerfully to its destination, sweeping smaller streams and forest debris with it.

Similarly, to be in the river of God's love is the adventure to which he has called all of us. God wants you to know this truth deep inside. You too are part of his purpose. It is really important for you to believe it and live in it. We can easily feel, because of low self-esteem or other reasons, that we don't belong, so we put ourselves on the fringe. That is not what God wants.

In this story, the scattered disciples initially witnessed only to Jews, so God's plan was restricted. But when other disciples started to share with the Greeks, and then Barnabas and Saul arrived, suddenly people from all backgrounds were being saved and filled with the Holy Spirit. There was joy and passion for Jesus and a desire to be taught and grow. It was like a surging river, flowing with such momentum that Barnabas and Saul were there for a whole year.

That surge was fuelled by the experience of being loved and chosen by God. We read that 'the disciples were called Christians first at Antioch' (v. 26, NIV). This mocking term became their identity. Because they were loved and included, they became like Jesus, with their practical actions as much as their words reflecting his love. This was demonstrated when Agabus prophesied the famine to come, and they all, independently, decided to give money and resources to help those affected.

Lord, thank you so much for choosing me and drawing me into the river of your love. May I be easily identified as belonging to you, Lord, because you have made such an impact on my life that others can feel it.

TRACY WILLIAMSON

Answered prayer

[Peter] went to the house of Mary… where many people had gathered and were praying. Peter knocked… and a servant named Rhoda came to answer the door. When she recognised Peter's voice, she was so overjoyed she ran back without opening it and exclaimed, 'Peter is at the door!' 'You're out of your mind,' they told her.' (NIV)

Have you ever cried out to God for someone's healing, salvation or deliverance, but hardly dared believe he would answer? This story shouts out the wonder that God works through our prayers to bring about his kingdom here on earth. It describes a dire situation, with James having been killed and Peter chained up in prison, awaiting trial, with many soldiers guarding him. It was impossible for him to escape, but 'the church was earnestly praying to God for him' (v. 5).

The church was praying. Like those disciples, I may pray earnestly, whether alone or with others, but fail to understand that through my prayers all the resources of heaven are being released. Do we see God as a tyrant who needs us to twist his arm? He is Father and longs for our faith to grow as we go deeper in prayer. On this occasion, the church prayed and God did amazing works in response. The angel came; Peter's chains dropped off; the guards were blind to Peter, and the very doors opened for him. Afterwards, he declared, 'Now I know without a doubt that the Lord has sent his angel and rescued me' (v. 11). We'd be in cloud cuckoo land if we thought that, as Christians, we shouldn't have difficulties. Rather, God wants us to be transformed in amazing ways even in the midst of difficulties.

The early disciples, even though they prayed earnestly, were still full of unbelief. When the servant told them that Peter was outside, they told her she was mad. What faith they demonstrated! But God was patient, wanting their astonishment and disbelief to become a stepping-stone to joy and trust. He is patient with us, too, and longs to take us deeper into the adventure of prayer.

Pray about your own or someone else's needs. Ask Jesus to help you to pray with expectation. Is there any insight he wants to show you? Thank him, for thankfulness opens the door to answered prayer.

TRACY WILLIAMSON

A rollercoaster lifestyle

They stoned Paul and dragged him outside the city, thinking he was dead. But after the disciples had gathered round him, he got up and went back into the city. The next day he and Barnabas left for Derbe. They preached the gospel in that city. (NIV)

The good news is spreading. The disciples are travelling, preaching the gospel and doing miracles. Nowadays, if we start an itinerant ministry, we may experience some difficulties while travelling or face being mocked for our beliefs, but such problems pale into insignificance when we see what the disciples faced every day. This part of Acts reads like a rollercoaster of ups, downs and dramatic interventions from God.

The passage begins with a lame man being healed. Paul was preaching the gospel to a crowd of thousands, but, as he looked across the sea of faces, God showed him that this particular man had faith for healing. Paul only had to call, 'Stand up on your feet' and the man jumped up, instantly healed. This reveals our breathtaking authority in Christ when we walk in partnership with him.

From exhilaration came the horrified realisation that the crowds thought Paul and Barnabas were Greek gods and wanted to sacrifice to them. The apostles 'tore their clothes and rushed out' (v. 14) and were struggling to restore calm when the Jews violently incited the crowds to stone Paul and leave him for dead. From glory to devastation in minutes!

Perhaps, when life hits us, we can't imagine moving on, but hopelessness is never the final word. Jesus is our living hope, as was demonstrated when God worked in resurrection power to raise Paul up, both literally and inwardly. Paul was filled with an amazing courage to go straight back into the city where people had just tried to murder him. His passion was to share Jesus. When we are that focused, we can ride the rollercoaster of life from a secure heart, knowing that Jesus is Lord and will work through us to reveal his glory.

Lord, thank you that you are with me for the ride, wherever it takes me. Thank you that you work so powerfully through me. Help me to keep my focus on you and not to be overwhelmed by circumstances.

TRACY WILLIAMSON

Keeping in step with the Spirit

They tried to enter Bithynia, but the Spirit of Jesus would not allow them to. So they passed by Mysia and went down to Troas. During the night Paul had a vision of a man of Macedonia standing and begging him, 'Come over to Macedonia and help us.' (NIV)

As a partially sighted person, I trust others to work out routes, especially at night-time when I may easily get lost. In the daylight I am confident and will blithely make my own way, certain that I know what I am doing, but quite likely to miss something important.

Most of us can see enough to find our way without help, but sometimes we live as if our lives are like a satnav destination. I make plans and then feel thrown if something unexpected happens. As this passage shows, though, we need to walk in partnership with the Holy Spirit, as God alone sees the future.

In this story we see God guiding Paul and his fellow travellers in specific choices. On the one hand they were stopped from going to certain places, while on the other they were given a vision of a man begging them to go to Macedonia. Because of their obedience, they met Lydia and her household, who all opened their hearts to God. How exciting that God is so involved in our daily lives—not to make us robots, but to care for and protect us and lead us to where we will be used most effectively.

Once, some friends of mine were in Northern Ireland and had just boarded a train at Belfast. It was the best train for their journey, as all the other options would involve making several changes. They were finding their seats when one of them insisted that God was saying they had to get off. She was so adamant that they did so, moments before the train departed. Hours later, when they finally reached their destination, they turned on the TV to hear breaking news: the train they had been on had been bombed by terrorists. How wonderful that that woman had ears to hear the Lord's warning, and obeyed.

Father, thank you that you lead the blind along unfamiliar paths. Please teach me to hear your voice and be willing to turn around from my plans as you guide me. Thank you for your amazing friendship and care.

TRACY WILLIAMSON

Thwarting Satan's plans

The jailer took them and washed their wounds; then immediately he and all his household were baptised. The jailer brought them into his house and set a meal before them; he was filled with joy because he had come to believe in God—he and his whole household. (NIV)

Paul and Silas continue sharing about Jesus. Wherever they go, they engender a response. It's not just what they say; it's who they are and who they love. This is true for us all. Satan's legions hate us to love God and will do anything to make us bitter, indifferent or afraid. But Paul and Silas' love for God affects the demon-filled slave girl, who starts shouting out a seemingly Christian witness. Satan wants to distract the apostles.

Have you ever been on fire to fulfil some God-given goal, only to find yourself distracted? We need to recognise and oppose Satan's strategies. Paul turns and confronts Satan, delivering the slave girl of the spirit that has brought her owners great wealth. Screaming accusations, these owners drag the believers before the magistrates. After a severe flogging, they are thrown into the prison's inner cell.

Satan seems to have the victory, but what are God's plans? He always sees the bigger picture and seeks our trust and worship even when things go wrong. Paul and Silas choose to worship, deeply affecting other prisoners. People are drawn to genuine worship.

This worship is sacrificial, as they are overwhelmed and in terrible pain, but they keep their eyes on God. Such heavenly power is released that a violent earthquake bursts the prison apart and they are freed. Instead of escaping, they reach out to their jailer, stopping him from killing himself and telling him about Jesus. He is transformed. Previously so violent, he now washes their wounds and joyfully prepares them a meal. Our worshipful love for Jesus brings about love for and in others, even those who wound us. Such worship and love are the greatest weapons we can use against the enemy.

Lord, my capacity to love you is so easily deflected. Please help me to worship and stand against Satan's strategies. I long for your love to flow through me at all times and to transform people and situations.

TRACY WILLIAMSON

The adventure of your own story

'"Lord," I replied, "these men know that I went… to imprison and beat those who believe in you. And when the blood of your martyr Stephen was shed, I stood there giving my approval…" Then the Lord said to me, "Go; I will send you far away to the Gentiles."' (NIV)

Paul is sharing his testimony. It is hard sometimes to remember our own stories and testify to what God has done for us, but Paul shows us how vital it is. Our testimony builds us up and helps us to grow in our faith, because we are mentally rehearsing what God has done for us. It is also a means of evangelising and encouraging others, as nothing communicates a truth more powerfully than a personal story. Think of the woman of Samaria (John 4) who, after Jesus had spoken with her, rushed away, saying, 'Come, see a man who told me everything I've ever done.' Virtually her entire community came to know Jesus as a result.

Testimony is also a supremely powerful weapon against the enemy. As it says in Revelation 12:11, 'They triumphed over [Satan] by the blood of the Lamb and by the word of their testimony.' It is in that context that Paul is sharing. Jews have accused him falsely; the protests, conspiracies, riots, beatings and imprisonments keep breaking over Paul like a tsunami, but he does not let himself be swept away by their destructive force. He is holding on to his own story—his faith history of what he was before he knew Christ, what Jesus has done for him and what Christ is now calling him to be. As he speaks, he receives wisdom to know how to confound the Pharisees and Sadducees and he is released. He then experiences God telling him to take courage, as he must testify in Rome. He can now rest in God's plan.

The memories of God's blessings can fade, but taking time to write down the key milestones, sharing your story with others and keeping a journal of your conversations with him or words he has given you, will powerfully enrich your life and witness.

Ask the Holy Spirit to be with you. Look back over a period of your life and ask him to reveal how he was blessing you. Jot down any memories of answered prayer or ways he empowered you.

TRACY WILLIAMSON

The adventure of divine purpose

'Last night an angel of the Lord to whom I belong and whom I serve stood beside me and said, "Do not be afraid, Paul. You must stand trial before Caesar; and God has graciously given you the lives of all who sail with you." So keep up your courage, men, for I have faith in God that it will happen just as he told me.' (NIV)

These final chapters of Acts reveal the wonder of God's divine purpose at work. He will use all that we go through, whether mundane, exciting, devastating or euphoric, in the working out of his plans for us. I would never have chosen a childhood crippled by abuse or to struggle with the disabilities of deafness and sight loss. God did not cause these things to happen, any more than he caused Paul's ship to be wrecked. He carries the traumas we go through and feels the pain of the sin that caused them.

Whatever you are experiencing now, he cares deeply and wants to encourage you, just as he encouraged Paul when the ship seemed certain to be destroyed, with all lives lost. He told Paul not to be afraid, that he had to speak before Caesar. Paul in his turn then encouraged the sailors and stood up to the soldiers. He was holding firm to God's promise and, when they eventually ran aground in Malta, they all saw that God was with them in the incredible welcome and kindness they received.

No, God does not in any degree cause our struggles, but he leads us through them into his amazing purposes as we open ourselves to his love. My purpose springs out of my experiences and pain. I couldn't reach out to those who feel lonely and shamed unless I knew the power of his great compassion healing my own life. I turned to books as a deaf and bullied child and he took my love of reading and enabled me to write words that transform others.

God is working in your life, too. Be encouraged by these stories from Acts to know that he is with you, and step trustingly into the adventure of your own divine purpose.

'For I know the plans I have for you', declares the Lord, 'plans to prosper and not to harm you, plans to give you hope and a future' (Jeremiah 29:11). Yes, Lord. May I not hold back!

TRACY WILLIAMSON

A whale of a time

Chris Leonard writes…

It's a great story, well told—and one I thought I'd known, backwards, from the age of three—but what is it saying to us, now? Researching for these notes—the floor piled high with atlases and reference tomes, Bibles bristling with bookmarks—has thrown new light for me on its message. Phrases and scenes from the book of Jonah echo through scripture, even in the mouth of Jesus, and Jonah's story, despite being set around 760BC, contains much that is highly relevant in our world today.

First, some background. Jonah, the fifth of twelve 'minor prophets' (Amos and Hosea were his contemporaries), lived and prophesied in the northern kingdom of Israel at the end of the reign of Jeroboam II and during the short reigns of Shallum and Menahem (see 2 Kings 15:10–22). All those kings 'did evil in the sight of the Lord'. Meanwhile, largely good King Uzziah reigned more stably from Jerusalem over the southern kingdom of Judah (2 Chronicles 26). Small states such as these would form alliances or fight wars between themselves, while remaining at the mercy of waxing or waning superpowers like Assyria and Babylon. Does that sound familiar? Think of recent events, such as conflict in the Ukraine and Syria.

In Jonah's time, superpower Assyria (capital Nineveh), though at a comparatively low point, still overshadowed Syria, Israel and Judah, demanding tribute, as indeed it did from 850 to 650BC. Archaeologists studying the Assyrian ruler Shalmaneser's black obelisk have found pictured upon it Israel's King Jehu, as he brought tribute to Nineveh. To subservient nations offering such tribute, Assyria lent protection from attack by other states. Those agreements were called 'covenants'.

I've found that unpacking something that seems at first like a fantasy—a fable from far away and long ago—sheds light on ancient and modern worlds alike. The same human frailties and the same amazing thread of divine plans link us with those distant times and far-off places. The book of Jonah has much to teach us.

The tragedy of a divided kingdom

[King Jeroboam II] restored the boundaries of Israel from Lebo Hamath to the Dead Sea, in accordance with the word of the Lord, the God of Israel, spoken through his servant Jonah son of Amittai, the prophet from Gath Hepher. (NIV)

Jesus said, 'Every kingdom divided against itself will be ruined, and every city or household divided against itself will not stand' (Matthew 12:25). The desperately sorry story of the Hebrews' divided kingdom, as told in 2 Kings, bears witness to the truth of Jesus' words. Do you sense God's sadness when his covenant people split apart, rebelling against him and bringing others tribute instead of relying on his love and covenant protection? Does that ring any bells for you on a personal level, too?

Again and again, both through grace and through punishments such as exile, God sought to bring both kingdoms to repentance and restore them to himself. The Old Testament's sole reference to Jonah, outside the book bearing his name, is his prophecy in 14:25. It speaks of the Lord being moved to compassion by his chosen people's suffering under their terrible leadership.

Lebo Hamath marked the entrance to hostile territory north of the kingdom of Israel, whose capital was Samaria. The Dead Sea was far to the south—so King Jeroboam ruled over a large area. Yet we read in 2 Kings 17:22–23 (only 50 to 60 years later), 'The Israelites persisted in all the sins of Jeroboam… until the Lord removed them from his presence, as he had warned through all his servants the prophets. So the people of Israel were taken from their homeland into exile in Assyria, and they are still there.' The Assyrian king brought in other peoples to resettle the land that had belonged to Israel. God's chosen, covenant people were reduced to little more than one of the former twelve tribes, based in the south, around Jerusalem—and issues with 'Samaritans' continued into Jesus' time.

Where you see division and bad leadership in churches or states today, pray for the leaders. Pray for unity within diversity, for people bound together by love under God's new covenant.

CHRIS LEONARD

Dividing himself from God

The word of the Lord came to Jonah son of Amittai: 'Go to the great city of Nineveh and preach against it...' But Jonah ran away from the Lord and headed for Tarshish. He went down to Joppa, where he found a ship bound for that port. (NIV)

It needs to be said with an American accent: 'You can run… but you can't hide!' Have you tried running from God? It's not recommended, experience tells me—though God is merciful. Convinced temporarily that Christianity, on which I'd built my life, didn't work, I once ran, on a bus, to our local city, with our two preschoolers. I must have pinned my faith on shopping. I can tell you that doesn't work, especially when it involves whining toddlers and no-show buses.

As a prophet, Jonah might have known that he couldn't divide himself from God or disobey his direct command to preach 500 miles north-east, in Nineveh, not even by escaping 2500 miles west to Tarshish (probably in southern Spain). Psalm 139:7 asks, 'Where can I flee from your presence?' Answer: nowhere—not even 'the far side of the sea' or 'in the depths' (vv. 8–9).

He was no coward, though, our Jonah. Most Israelites avoided the sea, fearing chaos, monsters and abysses. Boats powered only by wind and oars faced storms, unaided by rescue services, radar, radio, navigation systems or weather warnings.

We've read that Jonah came from Gath Hepher. It was a village near Nazareth, where Jesus grew up, and there are other parallels, too. Jesus slept through a storm in a boat. Woken by his terrified friends, Jesus spoke a word and all was calm (Matthew 8:24–27). Even the pagans sailing Jonah's ship knew that only God could calm a storm. In fact, Jonah didn't lack faith either. He believed what God said, but he didn't like it. That's why he was running away to sea. Maybe the most important thing we can learn from Jonah is that he was—and wasn't—like Christ. Yet God spoke with the imperfect Jonah and still worked through him, just as he does with you and me.

Ask God to help you discern where you're like Jesus, where he's taking pains to train you in that direction, and how he has worked even through your disobedience and frailties.

CHRIS LEONARD

Separated from the boat

They took Jonah and threw him overboard, and the raging sea grew calm. At this the men greatly feared the Lord, and they made a sacrifice to the Lord and made vows to him. (NIV)

These sailors honoured God more than his prophet did—and showed more compassion. We learn later Jonah fled from God because he feared that Nineveh would repent on hearing his preaching and would follow God themselves. Jonah reasoned that if he failed to be God's warning to Israel's superpower enemy, Nineveh, it would have no chance of repenting and would fall under God's destructive judgement. Result!

Jonah has so many good points. He's brave and he's honest, informing the sailors that he was fleeing God and admitting his guilt (v. 12). An effective evangelist, he tells it like it is in words that are highly relevant to his hearers, even though speaking those words puts him in danger: 'I worship the Lord, the God of heaven, who made the sea and the dry land' (v. 9). If Jonah (on whom the guilty lot fell) has disobeyed this God, then the sailors' obvious course of action is to ditch him. Jonah doesn't hesitate to give his life for the sailors. You could say that he opens their way to physical, and even spiritual, salvation.

God works several miracles, of course. The sea calms, the sailors discover the power of God, and man-overboard Jonah doesn't die because God provides a 'great fish' to swallow him. (When Jesus refers to the tale, it's a 'monster from the abyss'.)

To live and breathe three days in the belly of this creature could only be a miracle, however unwelcome to Jonah. Jesus called Jonah's experience a 'sign' of his own death and resurrection (Matthew 12:39–41). The difference was that Jesus provided access to grace for all through his obedience, while God extended rescuing grace even to the disobedient Jonah, Israel and pagan Nineveh.

Pray for any you know who are running away from God or feel divided from him in some way—especially that those in danger will find salvation.

CHRIS LEONARD

Reunited in the depths

'You hurled me into the depths, into the very heart of the seas, and the currents swirled about me; all your waves and breakers swept over me.' (NIV)

Down in the depths of despair. Plumbing the depths of depression. Mired so deep in guilt and failure that it swallowed my soul, my sense of self. Who'd want to imagine what it would be like to live three days inside a sea monster at the bottom of the Mediterranean? Yet many of us will identify with Jonah's state of mind, or know and have suffered alongside someone who felt like him—utterly helpless and hopeless.

Jonah's physical predicament can be seen as acting out some of the psalms of lament. Psalms 18:4–6; 42:7; 86:13 and 130:1–5, though not sung in the same foul and unusual place, all use similar language. Many who have plumbed the depths, like Jonah and all those psalmists, say that the worst part is feeling utterly cut off from God. Think of Jesus, crying on the cross, 'My God, my God, why have you forsaken me?' (Matthew 27:46).

Jonah's irony was that he'd been trying to escape God's sight. Through his redemptive 'punishment', Jonah learnt that, despite all indications to the contrary, God could still see and hear him. Even the monster had been sent by God to rescue him.

Some people joke that it was Jonah's bad singing that made the sea monster vomit him up. Seriously, though, his praises might well have been the turning point. Suddenly, in the monster's belly, Jonah realises that God can still hear him and he chooses to look again towards God's holy temple, to worship and obey. What an extraordinary change from despair to hope! Something similar happens in most psalms of lament, and it's supernatural. We don't have to climb out of the depths by our own efforts. Although his methods can be surprising, God *will* rescue and restore us.

Meditate on Isaiah 61:1–3. Jesus was sent 'to bind up the broken-hearted, to proclaim… release from darkness for the prisoners… to bestow… a garment of praise instead of a spirit of despair.'

CHRIS LEONARD

Together, mission accomplished!

'God may yet relent and with compassion turn from his fierce anger so that we will not perish.' When God saw what they did and how they turned from their evil ways, he relented and did not bring on them the destruction he had threatened. (NIV)

Having rediscovered his relationship with God in a dark and unlikely place and then been vomited up on the shore (we don't know where), amazingly Jonah was raring to go and preach at God's bidding. Nineveh lay a long way inland, roughly between the Mediterranean and Caspian Seas, near present-day Mosul. Today nothing is left of it but a mound known as Tell Kuyunik, 'the mound of many sheep'. There, archaeologists have found the remains of a twelve-kilometre inner wall, which could well have kept 120,000 people safe, although the city contained within it would hardly have taken three days to cross. Most scholars believe that description applies to its administrative area (think 'Greater London' rather than 'City of London').

Word spread fast. Just one day after this strange man of God had approached the feared and mighty Assyrian stronghold, the people believed in Jonah's fierce message and in his God, showing it by repenting in sackcloth and ashes, as people did then. Jonah didn't even have to speak before the king was following suit. Extraordinary! Scholars suggest that the Assyrians, because of their polytheistic religion, were open to honouring this foreign god. They believed Jonah because, in his condition, with his story, he was living proof of God's power and intent. We don't hear much about what Jonah actually said to these powerful people, but how we might speak the truth about God to people in power is a highly relevant question in our age, too.

It's worth reflecting on how God took Jonah's mistake, even his wilful disobedience, and turned it around to accomplish his original purpose—a miracle far greater than turning Jonah back from a ship heading in the wrong direction.

Reflect on how this ancient story shows God's longing not to destroy but to redeem, make good again and ultimately restore the whole world, not just his 'chosen people', to his original purposes.

CHRIS LEONARD

From the sublime...

But God said to Jonah, 'Is it right for you to be angry about the plant?' 'It is,' he said. 'And I'm so angry I wish I were dead.' (NIV)

Oh dear. We left Jonah and God apparently happy together in the last chapter, mission accomplished. It turns out that Jonah understands God really well: 'I knew that you are a gracious and compassionate God, slow to anger and abounding in love, a God who relents from sending calamity' (v. 2). How true! It would have made a great end to the story, but Jonah is still hanging around Nineveh, behaving more like a petulant two-year-old than a mighty man of God; still wanting his enemies destroyed, not saved.

At least he is still talking with God; in fact, they have a long conversation, and God isn't striking him dead. In fact, the bathos here is comic. Jonah focuses his anger on God for taking away a shady plant that he'd kindly given Jonah in the first place. You'd think Jonah would have learnt his lesson. God points out gently that he is more concerned for the ignorant 120,000 souls in the city, and even for their cows, than for Jonah's temporary discomfort. Was Jonah perhaps meant to have stayed on, to teach them more of God?

I'm glad the Bible is so honest. Few heroes of other holy books turn out as foolish as Jonah, getting things right in some ways and so completely wrong in others. I'm glad that our God still speaks with such people, teaching them, time after time, and not writing them off. Come to think of it, isn't my complaint that I'm cold as I type today, or my anxiety that I might be too hot at my computer in the summer, not just as foolish when I'm aware of millions of refugees living year after year in tents? Am I aligning my heart with God's or expecting him to align with my limited, selfish one?

Dear God, it's perhaps too important to me that my country, friends and family are safe, and that my life and home are comfortable. Teach me to reorder my priorities to come in line with yours.

CHRIS LEONARD

Together for ever

'A wicked and adulterous generation asks for a sign! But none will be given it except the sign of the prophet Jonah. For as Jonah was three days and three nights in the belly of a huge fish, so the Son of Man will be… in the heart of the earth.' (NIV)

Jonah's story has no satisfactory ending, it seems. What happened to him? He is never mentioned again, until Jesus speaks of him. As for Nineveh, the citizens may have repented and been spared when Jonah came to them around 760BC, but about 40 years later, when Assyria destroyed Israel, Nahum promised the utter destruction that we know happened around 650BC. Nahum foretold in three bloodcurdling chapters how God would rise up in anger against Assyrian wickedness and cruelty. The British Museum's Assyrian galleries show how terrifyingly war-loving they once were—yet how are the mighty fallen! As for the poor, ordinary citizens, it seems that, although they were conquered, not all were killed. Their descendants became some of the first Christian converts in Asia Minor, sending out early missionaries.

Jonah—and Nineveh—failed, succeeded and then, it seems, failed again. God sets a people or individual on the right track, only for them to fall right off it again and sometimes find themselves in a far worse state than before. In today's passage, Jesus speaks of seven demons coming to replace the one that has been cast out. We need something stronger and more permanent than Jonah's miraculous sign, even though it persuaded the Ninevites to turn from their wicked ways to honour and obey God, at least for a while.

We've seen several parallels between Jonah and Jesus, but pause now to consider how Jesus was in every way greater—righteous, obedient, powerful and compassionate. Jesus speaks of his own death and resurrection—the wider and deeper salvation through which God, at enormous cost to himself, would save his errant world. Ages roll on and he's not yet fully Lord of all, but he will be. Worship him!

Thank God that his new covenant embraces all his followers through Jesus' sacrifice. He is faithful, and, when we're not, he restores us and then fulfils his greater plan.

CHRIS LEONARD

Praying the Psalms

Lyndall Bywater writes...

When I was young, I was part of a church that positively encouraged children to take part in the services. We would often be asked to read a Bible passage or say a prayer, and the latter sometimes caused a bit of consternation. After all, as a seven-year-old, what do you say to God in front of a whole congregation of big, serious, slightly scary adults?

This dilemma was easily solved by consulting the prayer books. We had a few of them on our shelves—books of prayers that children might say to God, thoroughly vetted for any suspect theology, and laid out in rhyme-form with pretty pictures round the edges. You could always find something the adults would love.

For the next two weeks, we will be dipping into one of the oldest prayer books on earth. The book of Psalms was compiled about two millennia ago and it contains prayers written even longer ago than that. It is a fabulous cornucopia of all things human, gathered up into vibrant, colourful prayers to the living God. It is big on poetry but low on pretty pictures, and even lower on safe, non-controversial theology. It crashes its way through the complexities of love, loss, sin, sorrow, morality and justice; it plunges with both feet into the darkest of human experiences and it rings with joy and the highest of praises—and it doesn't put any of those things into tidy categories.

In other words, the book of Psalms isn't for the faint-hearted. It's certainly possible to read it in a faint-hearted way, skimming over the difficult bits and ignoring the verses about enemies being splattered on the rocks, but we're not just going to read the psalms, we're going to pray the psalms. We're going to look deeply into a few of those rather uncomfortable poems, eyeballing the bits that make us squirm, which we'd probably prefer to edit out, and then we're going to see how our own prayers might be shaped and deepened by these ancient cries to heaven.

The God who hears your prayers today is the very same God who heard these prayers when they were first written, all those centuries ago, and he is still listening. His ear is turned towards you as it was turned towards the psalmists, and your prayers are as precious to him as theirs were.

Apple tree aspirations

That person is like a tree planted by streams of water, which yields its fruit in season and whose leaf does not wither—whatever they do prospers. (NIV)

I turned 40 a few years ago, and one of my presents was an apple tree. At first I wasn't sure what to think of it, but as I contemplated the mountain of jewellery, clothes, smellies and chocolate that had been generously donated to accompany me into my fifth decade, I found I was rather inspired by that somewhat alternative gift.

With Benjamin Franklin's notable exceptions of 'death and taxes', it's true that not much in life is certain. There are no guarantees as to where life will take us or what it will do with us when we get there. Our ways are in God's hands, but that does not make us immune to the unexpected or the unpredictable. God promises us his presence and provision, but he doesn't give us an Ordnance Survey map of the terrain we're going to travel through.

The one thing I do get to choose, though, is what kind of person I want to be along the way. Like my apple tree, I am still growing. It's as if the writer of Psalm 1 is on the cusp of choosing what kind of person he wants to be, too. In the end, he settles on the image of a tree, plumbed in by its roots to an ever-flowing river. Trees don't come and go. They stay in one place. The tree he imagines stays connected to that life-giving source and never fails to flourish, no matter what season it's in.

My apple tree is big enough to sit under now, and it serves as a reminder that I need to stop drifting in and out, depending on the season. It's time to get those roots down deeper. If that's your prayer too, then let's see where 14 days with the psalmists will take us.

Spend some time today looking at a tree (preferably a real live one). What is God saying to you about your roots and your fruit?

LYNDALL BYWATER

Bigger picture people

Long enough I've carried this ton of trouble, lived with a stomach full of pain... I'm singing at the top of my lungs, I'm so full of answered prayers. (*The Message*)

Ron and his wife Lou were chalk and cheese. Lou had a 'glass half full' attitude, while Ron's glass was distinctly half empty. One day, on discovering that the freezer had accidentally been turned off, Lou was heard to declare, 'Ah well, sausages, chips and ice cream for tea it is, then', while Ron pronounced, at the very same moment, 'That'll be a whole new kitchen floor we'll need!'

The psalms can be a baffling read because their writers appear to live out several seemingly incompatible emotional experiences all at the same time. Psalm 13 is an excellent example: one minute we are groaning in sympathy with the psalmist for the unspeakable pain he carries and the next he's telling us he is singing for joy at answered prayer. So which is it? Is he in pain or is he joyful? Is he groaning or is he singing?

We can all be rather like Ron and Lou at times. We can get stuck seeing life from just one angle. If we're buoyed up on the positives, we don't like to think about painful things, yet if we're down in the doldrums, it seems like too much hard work to find the good in life. One of the first lessons the psalmists teach us is how to be 'bigger picture' people. As they connect with God in prayer, they let him lift them up out of their one-track thinking so that they can see the bigger picture of their whole lives in the light of his goodness.

Prayer isn't a download; it's a conversation. As we pour out our hearts, we make space in ourselves for God to broaden our perspective. As we look up to him, he shows us our lives in the bigger picture of his grace.

Lord, when my feet get stuck in the mud of my narrow-mindedness, please give me eagle's wings. Help me to soar above the landscape of my life, feeling the pain but also singing the joy.

LYNDALL BYWATER

Whole-life prayers

My choice is you, God, first and only. And now I find I'm your choice! (*The Message*)

One of life's glorious pleasures is having time to pamper yourself, isn't it? I'm trying not to make this sound too girly, but I really do love those days when I have the space to treat myself to a long bath, a thorough hair wash, a bit of nail polishing and maybe even a face mask. It's rare enough in my busy schedule, but when it happens it blesses me because I feel like I've given myself a treat from head to toe.

The psalms are wonderfully holistic. They don't just focus on so-called 'spiritual' things; they encompass the whole of life. In Psalm 16, the writer seems to be having something of a heavenly head-to-toe pamper session, taking time to luxuriate in the goodness of God as it touches every part of his life. He revels in God's generosity in providing for his needs; he stops to thank God for the place where his feet have been planted; he gives thanks for the stability and security he feels in the face of trouble. He rejoices in a body full of health, a mind full of revelation and a heart full of joy. He gives God credit for every kind of blessing, be it physical, emotional, intellectual or spiritual.

How thorough are you when you pray? Do you have a sorting system whereby you only bring to God those things that seem suitably spiritual? Do you sometimes feel silly talking to him about things that seem very ordinary? The God who counts every hair on your head could never be bored by you and he never considers your little things too little for his interest. When we include the whole of life in our prayers—everything from the tiny to the monumental—then our gratitude grows richer and our love grows deeper.

Could you have a head-to-toe prayer time today, giving thanks to God for every good thing in your life, from your career to your cat, from the hole punch to the health service? Be warned: it may take some time.

LYNDALL BYWATER

Hard-hitting prayers

O Lord, hear my plea for justice. Listen to my cry for help. Pay attention to my prayer, for it comes from honest lips. Declare me innocent, for you see those who do right. (NLT)

Engaging a solicitor to fight a legal case for you can be a great relief. No longer do you have to vindicate yourself. Suddenly you can drop the whole situation on to someone else's desk and they go to work for you, helping you gather the evidence, taking your case to court and presenting it to a judge so that justice can be done. Suddenly it's someone else's job to fight your corner.

The writers of the Old Testament often addressed God as their lawyer. Psalm 17 is one of many psalms where the psalmist calls on God to take up his case and fight his corner. I don't know about you, but I find it a rather uncomfortable read. It feels a lot like asking God to take my side, and history tells me too many stories of people who have done that as a way of justifying terrible acts. I get even more uncomfortable when the psalmists start asking God to wipe out their enemies for them. Is this really an OK way to pray?

The psalms are challenging because their writers don't hide things. When I pray, I like to formulate a prayer that is fair and reasonable, because I wouldn't want God to think I'm an unkind, selfish soul. Yet how often do my emotions tell a different story underneath? If we're honest, we have to admit that feelings of rage and indignation do sometimes flood our hearts. The psalmists weren't afraid to pour those feelings out before God, trusting that he would hear them, understand them and love them.

Perhaps it's time for us to stop editing our prayers. Perhaps it's time to express our deepest emotions, however ugly they look, knowing that our vindicator God is pleased to take up our case.

Do you have an uneasy prayer to pray today—something you're not sure God will approve of? Take courage and tell him; it is his job to bring about justice.

LYNDALL BYWATER

Celebrating you

I lead a blameless life; deliver me and be merciful to me. (NIV)

I am an avid fan of the BBC1 TV series *The Apprentice*, watching with fascination each year as a bunch of people endeavour to prove their calibre in a bid to win a small fortune to invest in their own business. It's always rather an emotionally mixed experience for me, though: on the one hand I am horrorstruck at how arrogant the contestants can be, while on the other hand I have to admit to secretly admiring their undaunted belief in themselves.

We don't take too well to show-offs, and that is one of the reasons why we sometimes find psalms like today's an uneasy read. Yesterday's psalm was the prayer of a man asking God to fight his corner for him, whereas today's seems to be the cry of an out-and-out self-publicist, calling on God to answer his prayers purely because of how well he is doing at life. He sounds a bit like the arrogant young entrepreneur in the boardroom, laying out his pitch in the hope of persuading Almighty God to grant his desires.

Yet I wonder if we feel uncomfortable simply because we have got more used to the other extreme. In our prayers, have we spent so long dwelling on our need for forgiveness and divine help that we have forgotten how to be rightly proud of ourselves? Have we become so reticent ever to speak well of ourselves, for fear of seeming boastful, that we have lost the ability to celebrate our achievements?

You have done well this week. You have loved and laughed, cared and prayed. It's true that those things won't guarantee you a trouble-free life, but they are worth celebrating, so don't be shy. Congratulate yourself on a life lived well.

Write your own version of Psalm 26, listing the qualities of which you are most proud, marking the faithful choices you've made and celebrating God's goodness and the good things you've done in the past week.

LYNDALL BYWATER

Hinge words

But I trust in you, Lord; I say, 'You are my God.' My times are in your hands. (NIV)

Have you ever considered the wonder of a hinge? If you haven't, then the chances are you've never tried to move a door that hasn't yet been hung. An unattached door is simply a very heavy chunk of wood propped against a wall, and it takes a considerable amount of muscle and effort to move it. A door that is hung on its hinges, however, can be moved at the touch of a couple of fingers. Hinges turn blockages into openings.

The psalms often come with hinges, too. Although translation hasn't always done them many favours, they were originally beautifully constructed Hebrew poems that not only expressed the writer's heart but also led the reader on a journey from one place to another. Many of them have 'hinge words' at their centre, phrases that turn the whole poem round to face in a different direction.

It's difficult to say whether Psalm 31 was written by David or for him, but either way it is the prayer of a man who has encountered all kinds of blockages. He is sorrowful, sick, despised and in pieces. Yet he has a hinge. Right in the middle of the psalm, when he has run out of words to describe how terrible he feels, he suddenly utters ten powerful little words: 'You are my God. My times are in your hands.' From that point, the psalm opens up into a celebration of the salvation that he knows God will bring.

Do you have a hinge? Is there a simple but powerful phrase that you call to mind when everything seems blocked and immovable? Speaking out truth doesn't necessarily change our circumstances, but it can swing our perspective around so that we can see past the blockages to find the open doors of hope.

Find a way to carry a reminder of your 'hinge words' with you today. When things start to feel impossible or immovable, speak them out to yourself and let them swing you round to a different perspective.

LYNDALL BYWATER

Learning to groan

All my longings lie open before you, Lord: my sighing is not hidden from you. My heart pounds, my strength fails me; even the light has gone from my eyes. (NIV)

A few years ago I found myself talking to a friend about a terrible experience she'd endured as a child. As she endeavoured to put her feelings into words, she suddenly burst out, 'I don't have words for it. Can't I just make a noise to describe what it was like?' I gave her the go-ahead, since that seemed an eminently sensible way to convey what she was struggling to put into cogent sentences.

Psalm 38 tells of one of David's less cheerful days, and it makes for dramatic reading. He really doesn't hold back in expressing just how terrible life is; in fact, I suspect that someone of my grandmother's generation might have told him to 'get a grip'. Our Western culture encourages understatement, whereas this most Jewish of prayers is all about gutsy honesty.

We've talked a few times already about how we tend to make our prayers too nice and theologically tidy, because we don't want to seem rude or disrespectful to God. The challenge is particularly relevant when it comes to expressing our inner pain and anguish. In theory we know that he loves us deeply, but in practice we pray as if he probably has better things to do than listen to our grumbling.

My friend found groaning to be a most liberating way of expressing her pain. Maybe you don't feel up to groaning just yet, but could you take some inspiration from the colourful imagery in Psalm 38? David felt punctured, crushed, dried out, sick and toxic. Which dramatic words or images would you use to describe the way you feel?

God loves to meet us in new places. As you pour out your feelings to him without restraint, you may well find that you hear him and sense his presence in new ways.

How does it make you feel to know that God loves to hear the most honest cries of your heart?

LYNDALL BYWATER

The in-between place

Deep calls to deep in the roar of your waterfalls; all your waves and breakers have swept over me. (NIV)

I was at a conference recently where the speaker asked us to consider which of our life experiences have been used most powerfully by God to help others. I thought about wonders I'd seen and testimonies I'd shared, but the answer, when it finally came, was quite a shock. The experiences God has used most powerfully to help others have been my experiences of unanswered prayer.

The writer of Psalm 42 knew a thing or two about unanswered prayer. His prayer is a mixture of devotion and disappointment, faith and frustration. He has lived through things that don't seem to fit with the goodness of God, yet he refuses to tidy his prayer into a cosy apologetic on why it's OK for everything to have gone so wrong.

When life fails to match up to our hopes and dreams, we have two options: we can re-form our prayers to fit comfortably around our experiences, letting God off the hook by rewriting the script to say that we never really had those unfulfilled longings in the first place, or we can use our prayers as the place where we wrestle with the discomfort of our experiences, challenging God on the disconnection between the things we've prayed for and the answers we've received.

In reflecting on the speaker's question, I decided it is my wrestling that has most helped others. I have always encouraged people to stay in that tough and uncomfortable place, facing the disappointments full-on and hammering them out with God. The psalmist describes the experience as a bit like being felled by a tidal wave, and that sounds pretty accurate to me. Yet, from that conversation laden with grief and frustration comes a deeper trust and a stronger faith.

'I will yet praise him, my Saviour and my God' (v. 11).

Father God, hold me fast in your mighty hand; help me to stay in that uneasy place between longing and accepting, contending and trusting. Teach me to wait with my disappointments until you meet me there.

LYNDALL BYWATER

Confession prayer

I learned God-worship when my pride was shattered. Heart-shattered lives ready for love don't for a moment escape God's notice. (*The Message*)

From the earliest days of the church, Christians have practised the discipline of confession to another person. It's perhaps less familiar to those of us in the 21st-century Protestant church, but we are definitely in the minority. For centuries, followers of Jesus have made it a habit to spend time with a trusted priest or mentor, talking honestly about their wrong thoughts and actions.

Theological positions differ on how necessary this kind of confession is, but Christians down the ages have certainly found it to be helpful and meaningful. They seem to have understood that our souls are healthier when we learn to be vulnerable.

Psalm 51 is one of the most well-known psalms in the Bible. It appears in all kinds of liturgy and song. Perhaps it is popular because it is such a tender and heartfelt prayer of confession. We may not like to admit it out loud, but deep down we can relate to David's feelings of shame and brokenness.

Sin is destructive. I often liken it to that moment when a stone hits your windscreen and the glass crazes. The cracks of guilt and shame shoot out, obscuring our view of ourselves and the world around us. Forgiveness is ours in Christ Jesus—there is no doubt about that—but sometimes it takes the hammer of confession to shatter the glass so that it can be replaced by something new and whole. We don't enjoy the shattering, but it does us good.

Do you need to make a confession today? Whether or not you decide to confess to another person later, why not start with a full and frank confession to God? Use Psalm 51 as your template, being honest about your sin, smashing out the old guilt and shame, then asking God to renew your soul.

Gracious God, give me open eyes to see the stains of sin in my life; give me an honest heart to own my wrong thoughts and attitudes; give me a willing mind to choose new patterns of behaviour.

LYNDALL BYWATER

The security trilogy

Truly he is my rock and my salvation; he is my fortress, I shall never be shaken. (NIV)

What's your approach to packing? Do you go with the chaos of spontaneity or the rigour of lists? My life involves a lot of packing, so I've countered the mundanity of the task by making it poetic. I have a 'packing poem' that covers all the essentials, and I say it before I close the case, to make sure everything is present and correct.

Checklists keep us on track. They help us ensure that we don't forget the things we most need to remember. It won't surprise you, then, to know that the writers of the psalms—who had a good take on what was important in life—were big fans of checklists. There are particular sets of phrases that occur again and again in their poetry, often at the beginning and end of their prayers, as if to keep them from overlooking anything essential.

Perhaps the most common checklist is the one we find in verse 2 of today's psalm. It's what you might call the 'security trilogy': God is rock, fortress and salvation. It's easy to think that these are just three alternative words for the same thing, but in fact they're distinctly different, and, as with any checklist, they all need to be remembered.

God is rock. He is the solid foundation under our feet. All around us may shift and change, but he will always undergird us.

God is fortress. He is the safe place that wraps around us when we feel vulnerable and scared. Whatever's happening out there, there is always a warm welcome in him.

God is salvation. He isn't just a castle we retreat to; he's a rescuer who comes to find us when we're in difficulty. He may be solid and firm, but he's also a passionate and powerful warrior who fights for us.

Is there a creative way to help yourself remember this Psalm 62:2 checklist? Do you have some jewellery with three stones you could wear, or something you could make and put on your desk as a reminder?

LYNDALL BYWATER

Lament for the nation

We are given no signs from God; no prophets are left, and none of us knows how long this will be. (NIV)

The reporter knelt at the roadside to talk to the woman. Her sobs made her words almost incoherent. Her child was sick with hunger and her measly possessions were all scooped up in one dishevelled cloth bag. 'Why are you crying?' he asked, in that way reporters sometimes have of asking for the blindingly obvious.

'I cry for my country!' It seemed so incongruous. Her own life was in tatters, yet her tears were for the war-torn land she had left behind her. The reporter was clearly perplexed. He had probably felt a bit frustrated at the machinations of his political leaders and he might even have felt the odd wave of depression at the state of society, but he had never wept for his country.

The second half of the book of Psalms is considerably more outward-looking than the first half. The writers pray large-scale prayers, concerning themselves with the epic landscapes of governmental justice and the destiny of nations. Psalm 74, like many of its predecessors, can make for uncomfortable reading. Like the TV reporter, many of us have never had the experience of weeping for our land. Perhaps we think that life in our land isn't really bad enough to weep over. The things that trouble us are often the product of our own greed and selfishness, and it seems churlish to bother God with them.

Yet the God who answered the prayers of the psalmist is still looking for intercessors. He is looking for people who will pour out their hearts in grief at the pain and poverty, the indifference and the injustice. He longs to save not just our souls but also our nations, yet he has limited himself to working only in answer to believing and passionate prayer. Are you up for the task?

What breaks your heart about this nation we live in? What might bring you to tears for this land? Take some time today to call out to the God who is just waiting to be asked for his intervention.

LYNDALL BYWATER

Story songs

Let the redeemed of the Lord tell their story—those he redeemed from the hand of the foe, those he gathered from the lands, from east and west, from north and south. (NIV)

The world of internet searching has changed a lot in recent years. Back in the days when the worldwide web was young, if you were fortunate enough to own a computer and even more fortunate to know what a search engine was, you would type something into the search field and back would come a whole host of encyclopedia-type sites with factual information. Nowadays, when you flick the search app open on your phone and type in your query, the first 20 results are likely to be stories from people who have been in the same situation as you or needed the same information, and have been kind enough to write up their experiences. In today's internet culture, we are more likely to learn from bloggers than from encyclopedias.

Of course, this trend is a return to the very ancient. For centuries, people have been learning from stories, and if you have a few good stories up your sleeve, you can convey a lot of wisdom in a very enjoyable way.

The Israelite people had learnt that they were more likely to go astray from God's ways if they forgot their history, so one of the temple worshippers' tasks was to pen story songs, of which today's psalm is a very good example. These songs would contain stirring tales of God's goodness to them in the past, and everyone of every age would be taught to sing them. In ancient times, if you asked for an answer to your question, you were very likely to get a song in response.

We humans don't change much. We still need wisdom and we still need to be reminded of what God did in the past, so that we remember what he can do for us in the present.

Why not start a 'Miracles' folder in your filing cabinet or on your computer, where you store miracle stories from your own life and the lives of others. Don't forget to keep reading them, though.

LYNDALL BYWATER

Soggy seed

Those who sow with tears will reap with songs of joy. Those who go out weeping, carrying seed to sow, will return with songs of joy, carrying sheaves with them. (NIV)

I remember a time when I hit a very low ebb. I felt as though everything I longed for in life would never happen. It was one of those times when unanswered prayer just left me reeling. I needed to take some time out with God to pray and find comfort, so I started some music playing on my phone and hit 'Shuffle'. After a while, I realised I was listening to a song all about how God asks us to pour ourselves out for him, even when we already feel empty. Suffice it to say, I cried my way through the song and thought it sounded a bit unfair. How can God ask for more when you've given all?

That song returned to me as I meditated on today's psalm. You see, Psalm 126 is actually a song of joy, written to express the wonder and elation of a people returning from exile, seeing their dreams fulfilled as never before, but in the final verse it is as if the writer wants us to remember that it hadn't always been that good. The celebrations had followed a time of much heartache.

Going out to sow seed when you're weeping sounds like a bad idea, doesn't it? I can't do much when I'm weeping, and I'd probably put all the seeds in the wrong place! I'd rather give up and stay home, but the psalmist seems to be saying that sowing seed in tears is a mysterious process that produces a precious and powerful harvest. When we sow the little we can, loving people and loving God in spite of our own pain and loss, then God sets about doing something miraculous with our soggy little seeds.

Lord, when I feel empty, barren and dry, sow in me the hope of new life. When it feels as if the seed I have left is feeble and spoiled, help me to sow it anyway, that you might raise a rich harvest.

LYNDALL BYWATER

Love letters

May he give you the desire of your heart and make all your plans succeed. May we shout for joy over your victory and lift up our banners in the name of our God. (NIV)

My job takes me to lots of churches, and when I'm there we invariably talk about prayer. I usually do a talk in the adults' service, but the children's groups don't want to miss out on the fun so they usually do a session on prayer, too. On more than one occasion, these children's sessions have ended with me being given a stack of prayers that the kids have written for me, and it is always a highlight of my week to read them. They range from the quirky (prayers that Mummy and Daddy would buy them a hamster) to the sublime—prayers that God would heal my blindness. What I love about them is that they are more rooted in dreams than in what I might call 'reality'. They are often bigger prayers than I am praying for myself.

I decided to keep Psalm 20 until the last day of this study because it is such a beautiful and faith-filled prayer. It's really a prayer for the king—something like a national anthem, perhaps—but it rings with such an infectious joy that it's hard to imagine it being sung at a formal state occasion. It isn't a dutiful song of honour; it's an affectionate song of love, and I can't help thinking that the person it was written for may have felt a bit like I do when I read those children's prayers.

Praying for people is powerful. Letting people hear the prayers you pray for them is even more powerful. We're used to the idea of telling people we are praying for them, but what if we also took time to tell them exactly what we've prayed? Maybe our words of faith and hope are just what they need to lift their spirits today.

As you pray for someone today, why not take some time to write out the prayer you've been praying for them, so that they can read it and be encouraged?

LYNDALL BYWATER

Isaiah: a story of obedience

Sue Rinaldi writes...

What began as a gentle sway soon turned into some of the most gruelling, body-shaking, brain-jolting sensations I had ever had the misfortune to experience. Soon, I was screaming at the top of my voice for someone to come to my aid, extract my terrified, rigid self from this instrument of torture and take me to safety. Obviously, the rocking motion of the rollercoaster was far too much for my ten-year-old self to embrace and the variable speeds made me sick. Needless to say, after that trauma, fairgrounds didn't feature high on my list of places to go.

I am certainly not equating the book of Isaiah to every part of my fairground fiasco and especially not to my plea for the ride to be halted. But as you bounce your way between present and future, juggle warnings of judgement with promises of hope and navigate your way through political observations and forecasts of salvation at the hands of a coming king, don't be surprised by the mixed feelings that may arise. Isaiah is a mind-shaking, heart-rending journey through disobedience, impending destruction and divine intervention from a redemptive God. It is also an incredible story of obedience and trust.

The name Isaiah means 'God saves' and every message delivered by this poet-prophet to the people of Israel, whether spoken or illustrated, identifies the futility of selfish ambition and the fatality of corrupt and godless alliances. Time and again, Isaiah calls for complete trust in the one and only sovereign God who will restore those who follow the way of holiness.

Born into an influential family with access to royal courts, Isaiah lived mainly in Jerusalem and began his ministry in 740BC. A privileged upbringing did not smooth his edges—quite the opposite. Isaiah spoke with the cutting precision of a razor blade, yet with the compassion of a man transformed by an encounter with the Lord's holiness. Isaiah answered the call to be a mouthpiece for God. Maybe there were times when he wished to be extracted from the prophetic adventure ride, yet he stayed true to his promise and serves as a great illustration of obedience. He did not put his trust in false idols, counterfeit heroes or humans, but in an eternal, exalted and almighty God. Prepare yourself for an incredible journey!

Live up to your name

For the Lord is our judge, the Lord is our lawgiver, the Lord is our king; it is he who will save us. (NIV)

When the removals estimator handed me his business card, I unleashed a smile. Robert Packer was born for the job! Similar responses may have been expressed when William Wordsworth became a poet or when Usain Bolt was acknowledged to be the world's fastest runner. I also wonder if becoming a weather forecaster was inevitable for Sara Blizzard or if bird conservationist Mark Avery would have cared for rabbits instead if his surname had been Warren!

An aptronym is a name that is amusingly appropriate to the person's character or trade, and there are countless examples. Actually, the Bible is full of them. Isaac, for example, means 'laughter', which is exactly what his ageing father was reduced to when he heard the news of his promised son. Fittingly, the name Isaiah means 'God saves', and each message delivered by this poet-prophet to Israel overflows with a complete trust in God's supreme ability to save. Even when exposing corrupt alliances or encountering idolatry or disobedience, Isaiah lives up to his name by repeatedly proclaiming the saving hand of God. It's intriguing how the meaning of Isaiah parallels his distinctive patterns of belief and language, almost as if his name becomes him or brands him.

Research indicates that people feel a special warmth towards their own name and this attracts them to activities that sound similar. However, many regard names as more significant than that, considering them as prophetic declarations or prayerful previews of destiny, with an innate power to shape the spirit and affect behaviour. Nowadays, names are not only assigned at birth. Creating passwords and user names for social media, gaming or online registration provides ample opportunities for incessant self-naming. Isaiah grew into and reflected his name, and serves as a poignant reminder to be mindful of the names we call ourselves and others.

Is there a name that you would choose for yourself, or that others have chosen for you, which reflects your calling and destiny in God?

SUE RINALDI

Grape expectations

'What more could have been done for my vineyard than I have done for it? When I looked for good grapes, why did it yield only bad?' (NIV)

Visiting the vineyards of California's Napa Valley was a breathtaking experience. The luscious sun-soaked landscape, bursting with clusters of vitality and promise, was the perfect vista to demonstrate the artistic and agricultural genius of our Creator God. Even though I am possibly the world's worst gardener and no plant is safe under my dubious care, I became intrigued with the way grapes develop. Left to their own devices, vines quickly become unruly and messy; they need to be shaped and trained. The pruning process is intensive and yet the consequence of cutting back shoots leads to the best possible harvest. In fact, the reward for pruning is growth.

The image of the vine is often used in relation to Israel, and, by way of a parable, Isaiah tells of a vineyard that only produced bitter grapes. The vineyard belonged to a loving owner, but, even though it was well placed and boasted excellent vines, the crop was wild and a far cry from the quality expected. The parable leads into a no-holds-barred condemnation of the moral decay of Israel and details the extent of God's judgement on a nation that has been woefully wayward and disobedient, celebrating everything except God.

Isaiah manages to portray skilfully that, although God is all-loving and eager for a productive harvest of right living and godly moral choices, there are dire consequences to acts of disobedience. The process of pruning may feel painful and look messy, but the only way for lives to produce great fruit is to yield to the shaping, training and nurturing hand of God.

Reflect upon the way God has shaped your life by bringing correction or discipline. Can you recall a specific occasion?

SUE RINALDI

Ticket to pride

In the year that King Uzziah died, I saw the Lord, high and exalted, seated on a throne; and the train of his robe filled the temple. (NIV)

My extreme irritation was impossible to hide whenever table tennis was referred to as 'ping-pong'. The term seemed to trivialise this ingenious sport instead of bestowing it with the honour it undoubtedly deserved, portraying it to a laughable knockabout, similar in status to Subbuteo or tiddlywinks.

Joining a competitive league was quite a commitment, and yet I embraced the opportunity in a way that would have made Clare Balding take notice. I was a winner. My sidespins, top-spins and smashes were the talk of the table and I swung my paddle with pride. Too much pride, apparently because the moment I became intoxicated by my own brilliance was the moment I started losing—badly.

Immediately before Isaiah's vision and hot coal encounter, we are told of King Uzziah's death. His fleeting mention is easy to gloss over, but, delving into his story, we are offered a cautionary note. Uzziah's reign was important to Jewish history and he started very well by doing what was right in God's eyes, bringing prosperity, peace and military victory to Judah. However, his later years were marred by pride, no doubt exacerbated by the acquisition of great wealth and power. Deluded by self-importance, he claimed for himself the right to perform priestly duties and was outraged when asked by the temple priests to stop. As he became inflamed with anger, leprosy broke out on his forehead. Afflicted and made to live alone, he was excluded from the temple until the day he died.

The proverb that says 'pride comes before a fall' can certainly be applied to Uzziah, as well as to my own sporting demise. It is one thing to start well, but to finish well is an altogether different matter and requires true humility and sacrifice.

Has your original intention to put God first been thwarted or contested by pride? Know that today God has enough grace and mercy to allow you to return.

SUE RINALDI

No regrets

Then I heard the voice of the Lord saying, 'Whom shall I send? And who will go for us?' And I said, 'Here am I. Send me!' (NIV)

As the helicopter approached, I frantically practised my 'Beam me up, Scotty' routine, which works so successfully on *Star Trek*—but, alas, nothing happened. Unfortunately, I was still on the golf course, about to fulfil a promise to my friend that I would accompany him on his first flight after qualifying as a helicopter pilot. Ever since 'Yes, I'll go' left my lips, I had secretly hoped he would never actually pass or that he would forget my uncharacteristic bravado. You see, I'm not a confident air passenger. I shake uncontrollably in my seat, always keep my shoes on to be ready to escape, and consider the phrase 'a good flight' to be an oxymoron. Climbing into the cockpit, my level of regret was at an all-time high.

I've often wondered if Isaiah ever felt a hint of regret over his quick response to the call of the Lord: 'Here am I. Send me!' After all, the surroundings were pretty spectacular, with flying seraphs proclaiming the Lord's holiness, foundations shaking and the temple full of smoke.

Yet Isaiah was not responding to the spectacle of the occasion but to divine revelation. Faced with the glory of the Lord, he was undone. As an angel-seraph touched Isaiah's mouth with a live coal, he grasped his true state, as a man woefully unclean and in dire need of forgiveness. Revelation changed him. It was from this place that Isaiah answered the Lord's request for someone to be his prophetic messenger to the nations.

Regrets? Isaiah may have had a few. His task was not an easy one but his willing response in the temple was not a fleeting whim or foolish boast. It was the result of an unforgettable divine encounter.

Have you made promises that you now regret? Ask God today to give you wisdom for your words, purity for your motives and strength for your journey.

SUE RINALDI

When trouble calls

For to us a child is born, to us a son is given, and the government will be on his shoulders. And he will be called Wonderful Counsellor, Mighty God, Everlasting Father, Prince of Peace. (NIV)

I am a Googleholic. My confession will not shock those who know me, because they often see me bent over my laptop, avidly consulting this 'patron saint of knowledge' for advice and enlightenment. One of my biggest flaws is looking up medical symptoms online: this cyberchondria turns me into a nervous wreck, convincing me that my mild symptoms have escalated into a full-on surgical emergency.

It is interesting to observe who people turn to when they feel troubled or distressed. Regardless of whether the problems are economic, physical, emotional or relational, there is a tendency to knock on as many doors of hope as possible to see what's on offer. The fear of impending doom and gloom can dramatically disturb the equilibrium of the heart and persuade even the most sensible to engage in acts of desperation.

Isaiah comments upon this type of behaviour and says that anything short of seeking God is futile. He particularly highlights the foolishness of idolatry in the form of consulting mediums and spiritists during times of darkness and despair, and affirms that God's sanctuary is available to those who trust in him. Isaiah then looks far into the future and describes the momentous arrival of Jesus, the truly great light who will establish an everlasting kingdom of justice and righteousness. This passage is often recited at Christmas time but is actually relevant all year round and provides great comfort to us in these often turbulent and alarming times.

American novelist James Lane Allen says, 'Adversity does not build character, it reveals it.' So when trouble calls, who do you run to?

Make time today to find sanctuary in the comfort of God's everlasting arms and be reminded that he is the wonderful counsellor and provider of incomparable peace.

SUE RINALDI

The coolness of foolishness

God told Isaiah son of Amoz, 'Go, take off your clothes and sandals,' and Isaiah did it, going about naked and barefoot. (*The Message*)

A Facebook status posted these words from a church leader: 'Let your dreams be bigger than your fears, your actions louder than your words and your faith stronger than your feelings.'

As I meditated on this wisdom, so many memories stirred within me of times I had allowed embarrassment or pride to stop me from doing something I believed was prompted by God. I recalled the occasion when a friend delivered a sermon to a large group of people in very odd, ill-fitting shoes. Her foot attire became the message, a visual illustration that proved both powerful and memorable. My initial discomfort at what I considered to be a rather ridiculous and extremely uncool exploit turned into admiration. She was prepared to follow the promptings of God rather than fret about how she looked. Quite honestly, my image-conscious self was deeply impressed by the coolness of the foolishness she exhibited.

Similarly, Isaiah became the message, albeit more dramatically than my friend, and his wholehearted readiness to embody God's words and warnings is profoundly challenging. In obedience, he threw off his sackcloth and turned naturist as a visible portrayal of the Lord's purposes and pronouncements. For three years, Isaiah was an unmistakable sign to Egypt and Ethiopia, alerting them of their impending fate at the hands of Assyria. They would be captured, stripped and thus put to shame, and anyone tempted to trust Egypt or Ethiopia would be thrown into confusion by their misdirected optimism.

To follow God's promptings may require us to step out from ourselves and find release from certain inner attitudes and fears that hinder and obstruct our willingness to obey. I am not advocating a mass casting off of clothing, but whatever message we carry must be more than words, and God may well ask us to take a risk or two.

When was the last time you took a risk and acted on the promptings of God?

SUE RINALDI

Prepare to be amazed

See, a king will reign in righteousness and rulers will rule with justice. Each one will be like a shelter from the wind and a refuge from the storm, like streams of water in the desert and the shadow of a great rock in a thirsty land. (NIV)

How many times do people admit to not being sufficiently prepared? Apparently, the main reason for failing job interviews is not a lack of gifting but a lack of practice and preparation. Athletes do it, teachers do it, pilots do it, chefs do it—they all prepare in order to achieve a good outcome. Even the great inventor and politician Benjamin Franklin felt it necessary to warn that 'by failing to prepare, you are preparing to fail'.

Many of Isaiah's prophecies contain cautions and forewarnings of judgement and peril. Clearly impervious to the need for adoring fans, he delivers these oracles from God with unswerving resolve, to kings, leaders and nations. In the midst of frequent condemnations, Isaiah repeatedly implores people to repent and choose right living and justice in order to prepare for future blessing.

It is possible that Isaiah was referring to Hezekiah as the king who would reign in righteousness, or even the far-future King Josiah, but this figure is also understood to be Christ, with Isaiah looking ahead to a new world order. Putting this conundrum aside, the most important factor is that a Christ-like king will bring spiritual renewal and, as a result, change hearts. Isaiah calls upon people to prepare for the outpouring of the Spirit—in particular, for the women of Jerusalem and their daughters to rise up and mourn for all that is barren and forsaken. This humbling preparation will make way for the Spirit to impregnate soil and souls in order to produce blessing and fruitfulness.

Isaiah's call to prepare is more than just a few encouraging words. It is a rallying cry to provoke an all-embracing change of mindset, behaviour and belief, which will ultimately bring a change of destiny.

Are you aware that God is preparing you for something? Consider how God is doing this and be thankful for all you are learning.

SUE RINALDI

Coming soon

'Here is my servant, whom I uphold, my chosen one in whom I delight; I will put my Spirit on him and he will bring justice to the nations.' (NIV)

There is something wonderful about announcing good news. I remember when my nephew entered the room with a smile the size of the Grand Canyon and told us of his engagement. I had never seen him so thrilled and so full of dizzy expectation. Other forms of good news may be a house sale or a job offer, a long-awaited pregnancy or a holiday opportunity; whatever type it is, there is always an accompanying sense of joyful anticipation.

Science suggests that we have between 35 and 48 thoughts per minute. That adds up to thousands of thoughts each and every day, and, if you are anything like me, those thoughts will be very diverse and extremely evanescent. Our fast-paced, hypertasking culture makes it nearly impossible to slow down and focus. Perhaps that is why 'mindfulness' has become such a popular endeavour, because it encourages single-tasking, intentional thinking and meditation.

Thankfully, there are calendar opportunities that facilitate a slowing down in order to pause and reflect. Advent, for example, provides us with a stimulus to carve out time in order to contemplate the approaching arrival of Jesus. One of Isaiah's recurring themes is the coming of Jesus—his first and his second—describing how this chosen one will not shout and slaughter, as great warriors are prone to do, but will instead bring healing and justice to the nations. Blind eyes will see, captives will be released and new things will spring up. As God's mouthpiece, Isaiah obediently and poetically stirs the people to focus and reflect upon this amazing good news.

Let us also take every opportunity to be mindful of the king who has come and will come again.

Are you able to carve out time during this Advent season to consider the personal, historical and eternal impact that Jesus has had and will continue to have?

SUE RINALDI

Beyond the comfort zone

'In the wilderness prepare the way for the Lord; make straight in the desert a highway for our God.' (NIV)

I must have experienced a common sense bypass when I selected 'Ballroom Dancing' as my leisure activity at college. There has never been one iota of foxtrot fancy or rumba rhythm in my body, so, for one arduous term, I was most definitely and hilariously out of my comfort zone.

Everybody loves the comfort zone—a place or psychological state that feels familiar and provides a sense of ease and control. Stepping out from this zone raises anxiety and provokes a stress response. This can prove advantageous if new areas of focus and performance are achieved, but it can also have the opposite effect. Too much anxiety, whether self-imposed or as a response to external circumstances, can lead us into the danger zone where everything looks bleak and overwhelming.

Anxiety is not just a modern-day condition; through Isaiah, we see God speak comfort to a similarly tense and twitchy population. Although this passage specifically mentions Jerusalem, it probably includes all those who've been exiled, so the God of comfort is reaching out to all of Israel. As well as conveying comfort, Isaiah's message promises forgiveness and redemption, because the foretold coming of John the Baptist will prepare for the coming of the Lord. As valleys are raised up, mountains laid low and rough ground levelled, a divine highway will be formed and the glory of the Lord revealed.

In the midst of anxiety, Isaiah announces the coming of a saviour who will care for his people like a shepherd cares for his flock. Their Creator God has not forgotten them and promises to help as they step out from their comfort zone, learn to embrace hope patiently, and find renewable energy as they wait for the fulfilment of God's purposes.

Allow God to speak words of comfort into any areas of anxiety you may be carrying. May the Lord bring you into a wide open space of freedom today.

SUE RINALDI

Promises, promises

'Have you not heard? Long ago I ordained it. In days of old I planned it; now I have brought it to pass.' (NIV)

'Promises are meant to be broken' is a phrase that has unfortunately crept into commonplace usage. Although it is a crushingly disheartening statement, many people would claim it to be a true reflection of a world beset by abandoned covenants and broken promises. For example, how many political parties have lost popularity and support due to unfulfilled pledges? How many marriages have fragmented and failed as a consequence of unheeded vows? Arguably, the art of faithfulness is an endangered practice, and it comes as no surprise to see how people have become sceptical of the ability of anyone, including themselves, to keep a promise.

City after city had fallen at the hands of Sennacherib, king of Assyria. When Sennacherib threatened to conquer Jerusalem too, Hezekiah assumed sackcloth status as a sign of grief and mourning and sought the word of the Lord through Isaiah, who entreated him not to be afraid because the Lord was in control and would deal with Sennacherib. In the middle of an overwhelmingly menacing situation, God makes a promise to Hezekiah, who, at this crucial moment, faces an important choice. Should he believe the intimidating words of a king who brings carnage to cities and turns people into captives, or should he put his trust in the Lord who promises deliverance?

Hezekiah chooses to submit to the Lord. Just as Isaiah has foretold, 185,000 men in the Assyrian camp are killed by the angel of the Lord and, in time, Sennacherib dies by the sword of his two sons.

Where broken promises seem plentiful, it is good for us to be reminded of the enduring faithfulness of God and to actively desire to be reflectors of that faithfulness—promise keepers rather than promise breakers.

Write down a few of God's promises that have been fulfilled in you and in your life. Now pray about those as yet unfulfilled and declare your faith in a faithful God.

SUE RINALDI

You've got a friend

'When you pass through the waters, I will be with you; and when you pass through the rivers, they will not sweep over you. When you walk through the fire, you will not be burned; the flames will not set you ablaze.' (NIV)

My friend was ecstatic when she achieved her lifelong ambition to face her fear of heights and do a tandem skydive for charity. After completing her intrepid mission, she joined the slightly tense group of watching friends and family, who had been holding their breath for what seemed an eternity, and thanked her professional skydiving trainer. She admitted she could never have done it without him. It was obvious that my friend's fear was allayed by his presence and by the fact that he was with her every cloud of the way.

On one level, fear is a natural brain reaction to a stressful stimulus: we have all experienced the racing heart, the rapid breathing and the energised muscles. However, on another level, fear can invade our mind and spirit, distort thinking, defeat hearts and seriously undermine our sense of self-worth. Fear comes in all shapes and sizes and no one is immune to its creeping and consuming nature.

It therefore comes as no surprise that the word of the Lord, through Isaiah, persistently targets fear. Recognising that his people have already experienced so much anguish and suffering at the hands of kings and armies, God showers and strengthens them with words of encouragement, declaring that they are precious and loved, handmade for God's glory and never alone. Whatever happens, God will be with them every step of the way.

We all need to know that God is with us, especially when we feel afraid or are experiencing tough and challenging times. We also find strength in the companionship of others who carry and sustain us through the mayhem and the mystery. Similarly, we help others. Love is the strongest antidote to fear and, in this passage, God excels in expressing just that.

Receive a fresh touch of the love that God has for you. Whatever today brings, know that God walks with you.

SUE RINALDI

Jerusalem's greatest hits

Burst into songs of joy together, you ruins of Jerusalem, for the Lord has comforted his people, he has redeemed Jerusalem. (NIV)

Many songwriters say that their best songs come to birth during times of struggle or deep emotional upheaval. Inspiration flows freely in moments when the heart breaks over issues of injustice or human suffering. When Isaiah calls upon the people of Jerusalem to tap into their own creative skills, he knows that they have a lot of material to choose from. He asks them to compose songs of joy to declare how the Lord has comforted them and that he is the true and only source of salvation.

Their melodies may not have outclassed Abba's blockbuster hit 'Waterloo' or Bette Midler's 'Wind beneath my wings', but the message is gloriously liberating: God reigns! Isaiah enthuses over how beautiful the feet are of those who bring the good news of peace and salvation and of how God has faithfully nurtured his people. Yes, there has been suffering, but God will continue to deliver them and the whole earth will witness his work.

Human nature has a tendency to wallow in hardship and find solace in misery, yet Isaiah does not accommodate it. For those songs of joy to be released, the people must shake off the dust of their doubts and fears and throw off their chains of captivity. It's time to rise up, look ahead and follow God.

Songs contain an incredible force; they motivate, empathise, convey ideas, transform hearts, stimulate action and stir the soul. Jerusalem's songs of salvation were destined to do all of those things and more besides, because they carried a message of the unfailing love and brilliance of a God who spans eternity and reigns over all. Now, that is something to sing about!

What songs are you drawn to at the moment? Reflect upon the themes they convey and see whether you need to include a few songs of joy within your favourite playlist.

SUE RINALDI

By royal appointment

The Spirit of the Sovereign Lord is upon me, because the Lord has anointed me to proclaim good news to the poor. (NIV)

Reporters were in overdrive when Prince George Alexander Louis of Cambridge was born at 4.24 pm on 22 July 2013. Every detail of his birth, weight and well-being became a focus for millions of people around the world who were enchanted and enthralled at the arrival of a future king. As Prince George grows up, all eyes will be on him and no word or deed of his will escape public scrutiny.

During this Advent season, we are presented with a wonderful opportunity to consider the arrival of a king, and this particular king is without equal. Matchless and majestic, supreme and sovereign, the focus of Advent is Jesus, who was miraculously positioned on earth to live out the values of God's kingdom. Because he became a servant, others could receive forgiveness and have everlasting life.

One of the most celebrated passages in Isaiah alludes to this coming king and yet it contains a powerful double twist. On one level, Isaiah is pointing to a time in the future when Jesus will read these verses in the temple and become the fulfilment of this prophecy. Christ is indeed the anointed one to whom this prophecy refers. The Spirit will rest mightily on him, and his message will carry a divine love that heals the broken-hearted, comforts those who mourn and releases those in captivity. It is also considered by many scholars that, on another level, Isaiah is talking about himself and his call to go and proclaim the expansive purposes of God.

There is, however, one further application of this passage. We have *all* been called and commissioned to be carriers of the good news and to model the alternative values of the kingdom of heaven on earth. Do not be afraid: we are not alone, because the Spirit of the Sovereign Lord is upon us.

The servant king came for everyone. Consider and pray for specific countries and people groups who need to see a touch of heaven come to their earth.

SUE RINALDI

All-consuming

'Why spend money on what is not bread, and your labour on what does not satisfy? Listen, listen to me, and eat what is good, and you will delight in the richest of fare.' (NIV)

It was a significant moment for Apple fans when news broke that the biggest Apple store in the world was opening in Covent Garden, London. The queue to walk through its pearly gates started at least 24 hours before the grand unveiling, and the first in line was Rose Williams, all the way from Pennsylvania. In a similar way, the response to endless clearance sales or Christmas fairs illustrates a seemingly relentless desire to shop.

The book *I Shop, Therefore I Am* (edited by April Lane Benson) studies the serious, often secretive, compulsion to buy. We may not be the type of person this book is referring to, but we may have woken early once or twice to beat the crowds or spent hours researching the latest must-have appliance; or we may have gone into debt to buy that new car we've always wanted. Have you ever wondered if we spend too much time consuming the wrong things?

This question is not only relevant to our consumer-driven society. Isaiah also touches upon the dilemma when the Lord calls his people to come to him alone for their nourishment and provision. With enough divine resources to feed the soul and an abundance of the finest food and drink to satisfy the body, why look elsewhere? Why spend money or waste hours of precious time on things that will never truly satisfy?

Isaiah sends out an invitation and all are welcome. Those boundless living waters have already been paid for and there is enough for everyone. However, it does require a commitment to pursue God and turn to him alone for sustenance and mercy. If we respond to this invitation and receive daily from God's bounty of provision, then we will realise that his heavenly storeroom is the best place ever.

Imagine those living waters and be assured that the invitation to come, drink and find continual refreshment is for you. Are you thirsty?

SUE RINALDI

Who do you say I am?

Diana Archer writes…

Who do you think Jesus is? You must have some kind of an answer to the question or you would not be reading these notes. When Jesus asked Peter the same question, it was a key moment in their relationship. The disciples had been with Jesus long enough to know that he was no ordinary rabbi. This one drew crowds and controversy like no other. He also taught truth, healed illness, fed multitudes, banished demons and sent his followers out to do likewise. I am surprised he waited so long to ask them the million-dollar question. Had they made the connection with the prophecies from the Hebrew scriptures? Did they recognise the significance of the kingdom of God breaking out in all that Jesus did? Did they know who he was?

The challenge for us is probably the same. We have been with Jesus for a while, some of us longer than others. We have experienced things that we never expected; we have sensed his presence in our lives; we have tried to understand more. We certainly know more about Jesus than we did, but who do we think he is?

As we explore a few answers to this question from the Bible, allow yourself to be open to new possibilities. We all have filters on our minds and hearts that mean we see Jesus the way we think he is, rather than how he actually is. The way we think he is affects absolutely everything about the way we relate to him, which in turn affects absolutely everything about how we live our lives. My prayer is that each of us will answer Jesus' question in a new way in a couple of weeks' time.

We begin with Mary Magdalene at the empty tomb of Jesus. She nearly missed the greatest event of history because of her expectations and tears.

Risen

At this, she turned round and saw Jesus standing there, but she did not realise that it was Jesus. He asked her, 'Woman, why are you crying? Who is it you are looking for?' Thinking he was the gardener, she said, 'Sir, if you have carried him away, tell me where you have put him, and I will get him.' Jesus said to her, 'Mary.' (NIV)

Who we *think* Jesus is affects the way we see him. When Mary Magdalene, overwhelmed with tears, stood at the empty tomb, it seems that she barely realised she was chatting with angels. She just wanted to know what 'they' had done with Jesus' crucified body. Her grief was absolute and all-consuming. When she turned from the tomb and saw, through her tears, the shape of another person standing there, it is not surprising that she did not recognise Jesus. After all, she had seen his dead and punished body. Seeing that body upright and full of life again was not in her range of options. Even when he spoke, she could not hear that it was Jesus' voice. Was he smiling as he waited for her to really see him, knowing the joy that was just about to flood her being? It wasn't until he uttered her name that recognition pierced through her despair. Then, she knew.

What an incredible encounter. It took Mary from the agony of bereavement to the beginning of a life-changing adventure. She could barely believe for joy—despite the fact that she must have heard Jesus predict that this would happen, probably more than once. He told his disciples that he would die and rise again (Matthew 16:21).

Everything we think about Jesus stems from this moment of resurrection. If Jesus did not rise from the dead, we are, as Paul says, 'of all people most to be pitied' (1 Corinthians 15:19). As we explore who Jesus is, this is the starting place: a cemetery garden in a long-established and contested city. Early morning revelations of hope beyond anyone's wildest dreams. A risen Saviour who has actually saved us, and, crucially, an encounter with him that will change our lives.

Dear Jesus, speak to me by name, as you spoke to Mary. Help me to see you as you actually are.

DIANA ARCHER

Is God love?

And we have seen and testify that the Father has sent his Son to be the Saviour of the world. If anyone acknowledges that Jesus is the Son of God, God lives in them and they in God. And so we know and rely on the love God has for us. God is love. (NIV)

John the apostle, who wrote these words, is someone who actually saw Jesus as he was, so we should listen to him. He lived with Jesus for three years—travelled with him, ate with him, talked to him, went to parties with him, watched him, loved him and became one of Jesus' closest companions. He saw him die and quietly asserts in his Gospel that he was one of the first to believe that Jesus had risen from the dead (John 20:8). He encountered the resurrected Jesus several times (John 20—21). He was filled with the Spirit. He features in Acts and he spent his life ministering to newly established churches in Turkey.

So when John says that Jesus is the Son of God and the Saviour of the world, he is talking about a flesh-and-blood friend. When he says that God is love, he is basing that claim on someone he shared meals with. This is not some airy-fairy, esoteric proposition. These are the words of a man who knew Jesus really well and testified that God is love throughout the rest of his life. This is solid truth based on historically justifiable happenings. John was an eyewitness.

Some of the Western world finds it strangely difficult to believe in a God of love, preferring to blame God for suffering and pain. Some of *us* find it difficult to believe at times. We trip up on the evil and hardships of the world and think that Jesus has forgotten us. Could it be that actually we are forgetting who he is? Forgetting the way he threw himself into that world, ministering hope and embracing suffering himself? Forgetting that he walks beside us, lives within us and treasures our tears?

Of course God is love. It's all about love. Listen to the apostle John and he will remind you and help you to see.

DIANA ARCHER

He was there

Simon Peter, a servant and apostle of Jesus Christ, To those who through the righteousness of our God and Saviour Jesus Christ have received a faith as precious as ours: Grace and peace be yours in abundance through the knowledge of God and of Jesus our Lord. (NIV)

Here we have another of Jesus' friends telling us about who he really is. Peter has moved a long way from that day in Caesarea Philippi when Jesus asked him the famous question. That moment of revelation must seem a lifetime ago to Peter as he begins this letter to encourage and warn Christian readers. He has been on a roller-coaster of a ride since then—through the arrest, death and resurrection of Jesus, through Pentecost and all the adventures of Acts. That initial revelation about who Jesus is has matured into a huge faith, which sees more and more. It sees that Jesus puts us right with God, that our faith is valuable, that grace and peace are available, that we can know God and Jesus and be known in turn—and that's just the opening sentence.

I have just had a phone call from a friend who is in dire straits about a family member in crisis. 'Does Jesus know?' she said. This is where the rubber hits the road. This is why we need to see Jesus as he is. Life is tough and we need a Saviour. In the moments of extreme pain, we need to be able to hang on to Jesus, even if by our fingernails. I know this sometimes feels impossible and God feels very far away. I have been there, many times.

So we need lots of truth in our heads and hearts that we can rely on in horrible times. Jesus is faithful. Because he is God, he cannot lie, and he promises to be with us always (Matthew 28:20). He tells us that the kingdom of God is very near, even within us. He is your best friend, so just turn your head and find him there next to you.

Dear Jesus, let me be one of those who has eyes to see you and ears to hear you.

DIANA ARCHER

Immanuel

All this took place to fulfil what the Lord had said through the prophet: 'The virgin will conceive and give birth to a son, and they will call him Immanuel' (which means 'God with us'). When Joseph woke up, he… took Mary home as his wife… She gave birth to a son. And he gave him the name Jesus. (NIV)

Well, I have managed to get so far without mentioning Christmas, but today is the day. Obviously the run-up to Christmas, which was originally designed to be a blessing to the church and to Christians, can be a stressful time of year for many people. It's a challenge to see Jesus at all amid the tinsel, hustle, bargains, preparation, school plays and all the rest, let alone to see him in a way that stretches our faith and understanding of who he is.

But please don't worry about it! The glorious, wonderful thing about celebrating the birth of Jesus is that birth is really quite ordinary. It happens all the time, even to quite young girls like Mary. Jesus came as a baby, just as we all do, and while some people knew his birth was special—people like Simeon, Anna and Mary herself—there were others who didn't have a clue. The shepherds and Joseph needed a lot of angelic interference or they would have missed the world-changing significance of 'God with us'. Because he is full of grace, God granted them those eye-opening moments.

So relax. Ask Jesus to show you where he is in all the bustle and busyness of daily life. Ask him to highlight people he wants you to notice and care for; ask him to teach you new things about himself through the ordinary, familiar—and sometimes stressful—routines of your days. Ask him to open your eyes to what he wants you to see. Jesus is not confined to Sundays or Christmas meetings. He is the sustainer of the universe, so he can probably speak to you through your to-do list if he wants to. Try it and see. He is Immanuel—God actually with you.

Jesus loves you so much. Let him share in your day.

DIANA ARCHER

Glory personified

But we ought always to thank God for you, brothers and sisters loved by the Lord, because God chose you as firstfruits to be saved through the sanctifying work of the Spirit and through belief in the truth. He called you to this through our gospel, that you might share in the glory of our Lord Jesus Christ. (NIV)

Here's another way of seeing Jesus: he is full of glory. We don't use the word 'glory' very much in everyday parlance, but in the Bible it is a pretty weighty concept. The glory of the Lord was in the cloud that led the Israelites through the wilderness (Exodus 16:18) and regularly rested on the tabernacle. The glory of the God filled the temple that King Solomon built, so much so that the priests couldn't actually get in the door (2 Chronicles 7:2). God is described as the King of glory in Psalm 24:8. The glory of the Lord is promised as protection when we are obedient (Isaiah 58:8). References to God's glory litter the psalms.

When the angels announced the good news of Jesus' birth, the glory of the Lord surrounded them and the very startled shepherds. We depict it as something shining, light-filled, awesome, extraordinary, brilliant, overwhelming. It must have been at least all of that—and Jesus is the Lord of glory (1 Corinthians 2:8), so that makes him at least all of that, too. However you imagine God's glory, it is outside our normal experience. It is bigger and better than the most glorious sunset and a million times more awe-inspiring. This is another side of Jesus—the one who is not like us, the one who is God, who is eternal, who is beyond our understanding.

Even more—because we are being saved by the Sprit working inside us, and because we believe, and because God loves us and chose us, we get to share in that glory.

'And we all, who with unveiled faces contemplate the Lord's glory, are being transformed into his image with ever-increasing glory' (2 Corinthians 3:18).

DIANA ARCHER

He is

'Your father Abraham rejoiced at the thought of seeing my day; he saw it and was glad.' 'You are not yet fifty years old,' they said to him, 'and you have seen Abraham!' 'Very truly I tell you,' Jesus answered, 'before Abraham was born, I am!' (NIV)

When I read about Jesus in the Gospels, there are just a few times when I almost feel sorry for his opposition party. I am sure that is very short-sighted of me, but this is one of those occasions. How *could* the Jews he was speaking to—or contending with—have been open to the possibility that they were talking to God himself? For that is what Jesus was claiming: 'I am' was a description limited to Yahweh himself (Exodus 3:14). This startling claim brought to an abrupt end some vociferous discussions in which a group of Jewish leaders accused Jesus of being variously a Samaritan, possessed by a demon, suicidal and self-authenticating. Jesus suggested that if they were real Jews who understood what it was to have Abraham as their ancestor, then they would recognise him as God. Small wonder that they picked up stones in outrage.

Yet I know that, as usual, Jesus was right. He had been openly teaching, openly healing and openly bringing signs of the kingdom of God, but the religious leaders were, on the whole, antagonistic towards him, with a few notable exceptions. Why did their hearts fill with fear rather than wonder? Why could they not see beyond the noses of their own carefully protected theology? Why did they not warm to this passionate, people-loving, truth-speaking teacher? Why, when he said he was the light of the world, the bread of life, the good shepherd, did they want to silence him? Why were they so reluctant to believe him? And when, oh when, do I do the same? When am I unwilling or blinded to the truth about who Jesus is because it is inconvenient or unexpected? When do I refuse to grow in my understanding? When do I not see Jesus even though he is standing right in front of me?

Lord, have mercy. Open my eyes.

DIANA ARCHER

Creator

The Son is the image of the invisible God, the firstborn over all creation. For in him all things were created: things in heaven and on earth, visible and invisible, whether thrones or powers or rulers or authorities; all things have been created through him and for him. (NIV)

How powerful do you think Jesus is? What sort of power does he have? This passage in Colossians tells us that we wouldn't be here at all without him. Jesus, as the image of God, was the initiator and creator of our world, our galaxy and beyond. He didn't begin when he was born in Bethlehem. He always was. He always will be. God is God.

It doesn't stop there, for 'he is before all things, and in him all things hold together' (v. 17). These are gigantic statements, with scientific implications, not just theological ones. Whatever we may yet discover about how the universe works, the Bible still asserts that Jesus made it and sustains it. Do you believe it?

How might these thoughts affect the way we go about our days? What does it mean to you that Jesus created the ground you walk on? For me, it's something about awe, perspective and gratitude, and I am very motivated about doing my bit for the environment—caring for the world that Jesus made. I am also ridiculously excited that I have a relationship with the creator of everything.

Yet it is also a very challenging thing for me. When the world presses in with its own theories about how it all began, do I still think that Jesus is the one who keeps the universe going? When my neighbour says that science has the answers to everything, what do I say? Where do I go to find creative and robust ways to defend and communicate my convictions? I have discovered some great Christian thinkers, writers and speakers who help me develop my own theology and understanding and give me starting points for talking to others. What do you do?

Is your Jesus big enough?

DIANA ARCHER

A to Z

'Look, he is coming with the clouds', and 'every eye will see him, even those who pierced him'; and all peoples on earth 'will mourn because of him'. So shall it be! Amen. 'I am the Alpha and the Omega,' says the Lord God, 'who is, and who was, and who is to come, the Almighty.' (NIV)

I have to confess that I avoided the book of Revelation for years. I could not make head or tail of it. It was the throwaway comment from a colleague that changed my attitude. He said, 'But don't you see? Revelation tells us how big Jesus is! And even better—we know the ending of the story. Because of him, we win!' Suddenly, rather than getting lost in the strange creatures, vistas and numbers, I saw what he meant.

The description of Jesus in this passage is nothing short of unimaginable. It is as if John is straining to find the words. None of them can do justice to the extraordinary revelation of Jesus that John has had. There is nothing bigger than Jesus and there is no one who can hold him down. He is magnificent. Nothing was before him and nothing is after him: he is it all. He is the Alpha and the Omega, the beginning and the end, and everything in between. This truly is a revelation, for, even when they saw him ascend into heaven, the disciples did not see Jesus like this. Perhaps the nearest parallel was the transfiguration, but even that was not on this scale.

On the days when life is frightening, problems seem insurmountable and disaster imminent, I need to know that Jesus is this big. Things in my life can get overwhelming for myriad reasons, and then I need to remind myself that nothing is bigger than Jesus, no matter how ghastly. This is Jesus who holds the keys to everything. This is the one who loves you to death and has freed you from your sin and has made you fit for his service. Because of him, in the end, you are on the winning side.

John's response to the majesty of Jesus was to fall at his feet 'as though dead' (v. 17). What is yours?

DIANA ARCHER

The Word

In the beginning was the Word, and the Word was with God, and the Word was God. He was with God in the beginning ... In him was life, and that life was the light of all mankind. The light shines in the darkness, and the darkness has not overcome it. (NIV)

It is easy to hear passages of scripture so often that they are almost too familiar, drifting over our heads with very little impact. These opening words from John's Gospel are a case in point, especially when they are repeated year after year in the Christmas readings. Yet they are dynamite.

John described Jesus as the 'Word' presumably because he knew it would appeal to the Gentiles among his readers. To them it would have meant the foundational wisdom of the world, the force behind the universe. Jesus is it. So that includes life—and not just a little bit of life but all of life, the life without which there would be no life. It includes light, in just the same way.

Yet, that life and light squeezed itself into one person, for us, for you, in order that you might become a child of God. So when Jesus says that he has come to bring us life in all its fullness (John 10:10), he really does have the authority to do it. When he says he is the light of the world, he actually is.

Christmas readings also remind us that the coming of Jesus was prophesied years beforehand. He was and is the fulfilment of all that God had planned for centuries and communicated carefully to his people Israel through prophets, priests and the stories of their everyday life. This big sweep of biblical narrative, or 'salvation history', began with Adam and Eve and found its ultimate expression in Jesus. Then the Spirit exploded the life and light of God into a dozen or so people, and a new chapter began. We are part of the grand adventure today, chosen and beloved by God. Your life matters. You are part of the biggest story there has ever been.

We are the ones who get to explore what it means to live with the light and life of Jesus. Enjoy!

DIANA ARCHER

I want to see

'We are going up to Jerusalem, and everything that is written by the prophets about the Son of Man will be fulfilled. He will be handed over to the Gentiles. They will… flog him and kill him. On the third day he will rise again.' The disciples did not understand any of this. (NIV)

There are things about Jesus that are very difficult to see. It is all very well for us with hindsight, but I know I would have scratched my head in confusion along with the rest of the first disciples. The Son of Man handed over to the Gentiles? Mistreated and killed? Did Jesus mean himself? Why would this happen? The disciples had seen him calm storms, feed multitudes from a lunch box and bring healing to dozens. How could a man with that kind of power be subject to Gentile authority? Was Jesus the Son of Man? Why wasn't he calling himself Messiah? Why wasn't he planning a revolution when he got to Jerusalem, to overthrow the Gentiles rather than be pushed around by them?

It cannot be a coincidence that the next story we read is of one blind beggar who was so desperate for his sight that he yelled until he got Jesus' attention. This man was physically unable to see; the disciples were spiritually unable to see. But when he asked for it, the beggar was given his sight.

There are times for us all when life suddenly takes a drastic turn. We were certain we were on the right path, but then everything falls apart and nothing makes sense any more. The disciples must have experienced exactly that. They were not expecting Jesus to be killed. It made no apparent sense. It was beyond awful. Everything in them resisted the idea that this might be in God's good plan—just as everything in us struggles when things are dreadful.

Yet God can bring resurrection out of pain, and Jesus still walks with us as we stumble along a new and often unwelcome road. Perhaps, if we ask, we might get to see why.

Dear Father, I want to see. I am asking, so please open my eyes to see what you want to show me.

DIANA ARCHER

The greatest to the least

In your relationships with one another, have the same mindset as Christ Jesus: who, being in very nature God, did not consider equality with God something to be used to his own advantage; rather, he made himself nothing by taking the very nature of a servant, being made in human likeness. (NIV)

Many Bibles set out this paean of praise to Jesus as a separate item from the run of the text. It is likely that it was a familiar description of Jesus that was widely used, rather than being simply part of the letter that Paul wrote to the Galatian Christians. Perhaps it was put to music; perhaps it was an oft-repeated creed.

It is a great summary of some of the greatest things about Jesus, encompassing his divinity, his humanity and his humility. It highlights the extraordinary fact that Jesus willingly laid aside his divine rights as Lord of everything in order to die a ghastly death for our sake. He literally stepped out of all that glory and into a servant's role. Not once in his three years of ministry did he pull rank over anyone. Not once did he demand that others serve him. He was always focused on the people he was with and the best way to love them. When he allowed his disciples a glimpse of his glory at the transfiguration, he turned aside Peter's offer to enshrine the moment permanently (Matthew 17:1–9). He spoke the truth about who he was, but he never insisted on personal worship.

It is this servant-hearted attitude that Paul wants us to copy. He wants us to treat each other in the family of God with the same kind of love and respect that Jesus had. He wants us to step out of our secret longings for approval and attention, and into serving one another's needs instead. If we all did that, no one would go unnoticed or unappreciated anyway, and our Christian communities would shine with such love and joy that Jesus would be glorified in the way he deserves.

Do you trust God enough for your needs that you can reach out to meet the needs of others? Jesus did.

DIANA ARCHER

Some things never change

God has said, 'Never will I leave you; never will I forsake you.' So we say with confidence, 'The Lord is my helper; I will not be afraid. What can mere mortals do to me?'... Jesus Christ is the same yesterday and today and for ever. (NIV)

The phrase 'Jesus Christ is the same yesterday, today and for ever' is often quoted and there are good reasons for that. It appears in the middle of the closing remarks of the letter to the Hebrews, where it seems that the writer is throwing down all the things he really wants everyone to remember. It's a final 'look-after-each-other', 'look-after-your-leaders', trust-in-God-today-and-in-the-future' finish to his letter. This seems to cover it all, really, and it is based on the firm foundation that Jesus will never change and has never changed. He will always be with you and always be *for* you.

What does that mean to you? We all have our strengths and weaknesses, our good days and bad days, our faith in Jesus and our doubts, but Jesus never changes. We have baggage from the past that we keep bumping up against, and fears for the future that we find difficult to let go of, but Jesus never changes. We worry about family, health and money, but Jesus never changes. We have courage one day and none the next, but Jesus never changes.

Give yourself a treat: make the connections between the challenges of your life and the ultimate, unchanging, reliable nature of God. No matter who you are or what are your struggles and joys, Jesus loves you the same all the time. He invites you to build on the bedrock of that security and let him in to all aspects of your life. He is God. No matter what you face, he can face it with you.

Look after each other. Look after your leaders. Trust in God. Jesus is always the same. Build on the rock.

DIANA ARCHER

Messiah

The woman said, 'I know that Messiah' (called Christ) 'is coming. When he comes, he will explain everything to us.' Then Jesus declared, 'I, the one speaking to you—I am he.' Just then his disciples returned and were surprised to find him talking with a woman. (NIV)

Don't you love the ordinariness of the Gospel stories? Even in John, who is sometimes accused of being less 'earthy' than the other Gospel writers, there is this glorious juxtaposition of Jesus' unusually specific revelation of his identity with the disciples' reaction to his talking to a woman. You would have thought they might have picked up the significance of the moment, but no, all they saw was Jesus trampling cheerfully over yet another social taboo. They missed the important bit.

Had they been a little more open to what was happening, they might have pressed Jesus to explain what 'Messiah' meant and thus saved themselves a lot of future heartache. As it was, it was the woman—out in the midday sun, avoiding the stares of neighbours, aware she was a bit of an outcast—who took Jesus on and pushed him for answers. So she gets the credit for asking theological questions and seeing that what Jesus said about himself was true. She was the one who believed in him and then ignored some social conventions herself, as she dashed into town to spread the news that she may just have met the Messiah.

Don't let anyone put you down because of their expectations or the way things have always been done. Don't let anyone put you down because you are a woman. Don't put yourself down, either. Jesus doesn't. The Samaritan woman (don't you wish we knew her name?) led her whole town to believe in Jesus. Through the testimony of this one woman, hundreds of people came to see that he was the Saviour of the world (v. 42). Who knows what you could do? Go for it!

Her encounter with Jesus began with a drink of water. Where does yours begin?

DIANA ARCHER

Life and soul of the party

On the third day a wedding took place at Cana in Galilee... When the wine was gone, Jesus' mother said to him, 'They have no more wine.' 'Woman, why do you involve me?' Jesus replied. 'My hour has not yet come.' His mother said to the servants, 'Do whatever he tells you.' (NIV)

This is the very first miracle of Jesus that John records in his Gospel. It is without doubt one of my favourite stories, and one that I come back to when I think about who Jesus is.

He is the party-giver. As well as being the Saviour of the world, the ultimate Creator, the fulfilment of prophecy, Messiah, unchanging, he is also the one who brings the party to life. This story of Jesus turning water into wine is echoed in the many parallels he draws between the kingdom of God and parties, banquets, wedding feasts and celebrations. His mum knew. She must have done: she was the one who asked him to save the day. She was totally confident in sending the servants to him for instructions. She knew he cared about joy and fun and creating wonderful times together. She knew he would not do it by halves either; she can't have been surprised that this water-into-wine was the best flavour of the night.

This is what the kingdom of God is like. This is what the king of the kingdom is like. This is who he is: the author of life, the inventor of goodness and truth, the rescuer, the healer and the thrower of parties. These are the sort of parties where no one feels left out, shy, worried about looking right or nervous about chatting. The divine party-giver has invited us personally, chosen the outfits, wiped away our tears, made us shine with the beauty of being totally loved, and laid out a feast perfectly suited for all. The glimpses we get now of who Jesus is are nothing compared to the whole picture, which we will see.

We might as well look forward to it. The best is yet to come!

DIANA ARCHER

Christmas characters

Jill Rattle writes…

I wonder whether I, writing these words so far in advance of Christmas, will be doing what you are doing today—stopping to spend a little while encountering Jesus through the scriptures. I'd like to think I will make the same choice as you. Unless your circumstances are rather different from the norm, you are probably really busy, possibly tired, even a bit stressed and wondering how you'll get everything done in time for the Big Day—and still you have made time for Jesus. He is pleased you are 'sitting at his feet' and wanting to hear from him, learn from him and just be near him.

I'm reminded of the time when Jesus was visiting his friends, Martha and Mary. One sister, Martha, was dizzy with rushing around, providing hospitality, while the other, Mary, sat enthralled at Jesus' feet, taking in his every word.

You are being a 'Mary' and Jesus affirms you as he affirmed her. It's not that he didn't delight in his friend, Martha, too. He appreciated her loving hospitality, her desire to serve him and her hard work, but right at that moment he needed her to stop. She was wearing herself out, gone into overdrive, ironing the dusters. (Well, the scriptures don't say that, but I bet she was!) 'Stop, Martha!' Jesus was saying to her. 'You need to join Mary right now, to receive all that I have to give you—and especially my peace.'

Jesus needs us all to stop from time to time and just 'be' in his presence. He is speaking to us those wonderful words, 'Come, all of you who are weary and heavy laden, and I will give you rest.' The resting period does not last for ever. It's not meant to: it's the prelude to service. Once you've done the most important thing you can do—worship Jesus—you will find you have the grace and strength to serve others for him.

Isaiah predicts Jesus' coming

The wolf will romp with the lamb, the leopard sleep with the kid. Calf and lion will eat from the same trough, and a little child will tend them. (*The Message*)

Search for 'unlikely animal friendships' on the internet and you'll get a gallery of extraordinary photos: a cat and an owl hugging, a giant tortoise and hippo sleeping together, a mouse riding on a frog. Of course, the reason these photos are displayed is that the friendships look so unnatural and unexpected.

Isaiah has his own list of unlikely liaisons: the wolf, instead of devouring the lamb, is playing with it; the predatory leopard and a defenceless kid sleep peacefully together; the lion is sharing his (vegetarian) meal with a calf. Most unlikely, we might think—but in his vision, Isaiah sees the world no longer divided into oppressor and oppressed, attacker and victim. It is at peace, in harmony. 'And a little child will tend them': Isaiah foretells the coming of the Prince of Peace who will usher in a kingdom of unity, where loving relationships replace old divisions and hatred, where there are no victims and all are equal.

Jesus came, as a baby, to fulfil that prophecy and establish his new kingdom of heaven on earth. He came into a world where Caesar's might crushed his enemies, where Jews and Gentiles were divided and religious leaders led their people into bondage, not freedom. Jesus came to establish a new way, the way of peace. It took him to the cross, which seemed like a defeat, but three days later his resurrection won the greatest victory of all time.

As we look around our world, we see that Jesus' kingdom of heaven is here, but not yet complete. The kingdom of 'Caesar' is still very apparent, as wars rage, terrorism terrifies and even the church, which is Christ's body, is torn by division. *But*, and it's a glorious 'but', one day Jesus will return and Isaiah's vision will be reality.

Consider the ways in which you can be a 'peacemaker' in your everyday life, cooperating with the Lord in building his kingdom of love and peace.

JILL RATTLE

Joseph

An angel appeared to him in a dream and said, 'Joseph son of David, do not be afraid to take Mary home as your wife, because what is conceived in her is from the Holy Spirit.' (NIV)

When King Richard III's remains were reburied in Leicester, his coffin was made by a male descendant of the royal line who was not a prince or a nobleman, but a carpenter. Ordinary people sometimes have royal ancestry.

Do you think Joseph, the humble carpenter, thought much about his incredibly famous lineage, laid out in Matthew 1? He could trace his direct line back through King David to Abraham. He himself was of no particular consequence or rank: he was a very ordinary Jew, living a very ordinary life. He probably didn't have great expectations for his future other than pleasure at the prospect of marrying his beautiful fiancée and their undoubted happy life together.

Suddenly, though, the extraordinary breaks into his ordinary life. A divine visitor tells him in a dream that he is to be the adoptive father of the child soon to be born to his virgin bride. Shock! The angel then asks Joseph to accept that this event, which his community will judge a social disaster and disgrace, is the world-changing work of the Holy Spirit. As Joseph's adopted child Jesus would legally inherit the same family line, he would be the son of Abraham and son of David—but, far more than that, he would be the Son of God, the long-awaited Messiah.

What a lot for a humble carpenter to take in! His reaction shows that he was far from ordinary; he was a man of extraordinary faith and trust. God had spoken and he would obey. He willingly set out on a path to protect and nurture the amazing child that God had entrusted to him and his wife. An ordinary life, placed at God's disposal, became an important part of God's plan.

Lord, help me to follow Joseph's example and place my life at your disposal.

JILL RATTLE

Mary says 'yes'

The angel answered, 'The Holy Spirit will come on you, and the power of the Most High will overshadow you. So the holy one to be born will be called the Son of God…' 'I am the Lord's servant,' Mary answered. 'May your word to me be fulfilled.' (NIV)

Mary was a humble Jewish girl, but, like her carpenter husband, she could trace her ancestry back to King David. Her son, Jesus, as foretold in the Old Testament, was the Messiah born into the royal line. But although Mary occupied a low rank in society, like Joseph she really can't be described as 'ordinary'. Her reaction to the angel's visitation is extraordinary.

In the Old Testament, those called by God to undertake a challenging task often demurred and needed persuading: Moses wanted God to choose someone else, Gideon was terrified and needed a sign, Isaiah wallowed in his 'wretchedness', Jeremiah protested his youth and Jonah went to extreme lengths to avoid his calling. Me? I often demur when I think God wants me to do something hard.

Mary listens to the angel: 'May your word to me be fulfilled,' she says simply. One writer imagines the heavenly hosts watching this scene, waiting with bated breath for Mary's reply. Will she say 'yes'? Given her free will, she could have said 'no', but God knew this girl's heart; he knew her love for him, her courage, her openness to his Spirit. Gabriel greets her: 'You're beautiful with God's beauty' (v. 28, *The Message*). She might be lowly in society's eyes, but in God's eyes she is the perfect choice to be the mother of his beloved Son.

God doesn't present us with anything as challenging as Mary faced, but when he does ask us to do something for him, perhaps outside our comfort zone, will we be ready to say 'yes'? We are assured of the Holy Spirit's help if we do.

Lord, whatever tasks you have for me, whether small or big, give me the grace to say 'yes' and to trust your Holy Spirit to carry me through.

JILL RATTLE

Elizabeth: surprised by joy

Elizabeth became pregnant and for five months remained in seclusion. 'The Lord has done this for me,' she said.' (NIV)

Recently I rejoiced with a member of our church who has, in her early 50s, given birth to her first child. Wonderfully but perhaps not surprisingly, she has called him Samuel—'asked of God; heard by God'—recalling Hannah's experience in the Old Testament.

Elizabeth was much older than my friend and had no children. She, as well as her priest husband Zechariah, was a descendant of the priestly line of Aaron, but the line was to stop with them. Elizabeth had never been able to conceive and now she was past menopause. Like many women before and now, that was hard for her to deal with, made worse by a society that considered childlessness a disgrace.

From her husband's shock encounter with an angel in the temple, it seems they had been praying for many years ('Do not be afraid', says the angel; 'your prayer has been heard'), but when the promise came, Zechariah couldn't quite believe it and was struck dumb.

Yet it was true: God's plan for his Son's coming to earth involved Elizabeth as well as her much younger cousin, Mary. For them both, what was impossible in human terms was possible with God: Mary would experience virgin birth, Elizabeth pregnancy in old age. I wonder if, as Elizabeth felt the first stirrings of new life within her, she thought back to Hannah and, before her, to Sarah, wife of Abraham, who conceived Isaac in old age. Perhaps she wondered initially whether to call her baby Samuel or even Isaac, but Zechariah had been told by the angel that his name should be John: 'Jehovah is gracious'.

I love the way the angel tells Zechariah that the baby would be 'a joy and delight to you' (v. 14). Our God is a God of joyful surprises.

Jehovah is gracious. Yes, he is! God has a different loving plan for each one of us—and he will surprise us with joy.

JILL RATTLE

Elizabeth and Mary

When Elizabeth heard Mary's greeting, the baby leaped in her womb, and Elizabeth was filled with the Holy Spirit. (NIV)

I looked for a spare seat in the crowded café on the lip of the Grand Canyon. Two women gestured that I could join them at their table. Within minutes we had established that we were all Christians and there was an instant rapport as we recognised the Spirit of Jesus within each other. Although we would probably never see each other again, for that short time there was delight in fellowship. Have you had a similar heart-warming experience? You meet a stranger and, because both of you have the Spirit of Jesus within, you feel you are 'family'.

Mary and Elizabeth, of course, were not strangers; they were cousins. But when they met, six months into Elizabeth's pregnancy, something amazing and beautiful happened: the baby John, still in Elizabeth's womb, leapt for joy, and Elizabeth herself was filled with the Holy Spirit. The Bible says that she 'sang out exuberantly, "You're so blessed among women, and the babe in your womb, also blessed!' (v. 42, *The Message*). Mother and unborn baby both responded to the presence of Jesus within the womb of his mother, Mary.

What an encounter! Both women already knew that God was working within them, but, when they met, affirmation and assurance burst out in uncontainable joy (we'll look at Mary's reaction tomorrow). Elizabeth had been told that her son would be great. Indeed, Jesus later told people that John was the greatest man ever born, up to that point in history (Luke 7:28).

Elizabeth knew, however, that the one whom Mary carried would be far greater, and she called Mary's unborn child 'my Lord'. Does that make Elizabeth the first disciple of Jesus, I wonder? Certainly, what marks out the believer from the non-believer is that the believer can say, 'Jesus is my Lord.' Elizabeth knew for certain that the Saviour had come.

Do you meet regularly for prayer and support with another woman? If not, perhaps you can think about it. It is such a joy, a privilege and an affirmation of your mutual faith.

JILL RATTLE

Mary's worship song (1)

'My soul glorifies the Lord and my spirit rejoices in God my Saviour.' (NIV)

A member of my family is a writer of worship songs. He would be the first to acknowledge that those songs will not be vehicles for authentic worship unless they are inspired by the Holy Spirit. It is wonderful that the Holy Spirit continues today to give words and music to his people so that we can better explore, experience and celebrate the heart of God.

One of the greatest worship songs ever written, if not the greatest, was the one the Holy Spirit put into Mary's mouth as her cousin Elizabeth proclaimed the presence of the Saviour within her womb. Mary's song is an explosion of praise to her mighty God. It has strong echoes of Hannah's song of exaltation at her pregnancy (1 Samuel 2:1–10), which begins, 'My heart rejoices in the Lord; in the Lord my horn is lifted high.' There is a marked difference in tone, though, between Hannah's song and Mary's, which *The Message* brings out sharply.

Hannah sings, 'I'm bursting with God-news! I'm walking on air. I'm laughing at my rivals. I'm dancing my salvation.' Mary sings, 'I'm bursting with God-news. I'm dancing the song of my Saviour God.' Hannah crows over her enemies: in her delight at her pregnancy, she praises God, but can't help looking around with a touch of malice at those who were previously so unkind to her. Mary looks in one direction only, to the God who has been so kind to her, and she is humbled by his favour: 'The Mighty One has done great things for me—holy is his name' (v. 49).

Mary is amazed by the realisation that generations to come will know who she is and the part she played in God's plan to rescue humanity. Joy, awe, gratitude and humility are at the heart of her worship.

We may not all be songwriters but we can invite the Holy Spirit to help us speak aloud words of gratitude to God for all he has done for us. Perhaps we can write them down as a record of his goodness.

JILL RATTLE

Mary's worship song (2)

The Mighty One has done great things for me—holy is his name. His mercy extends to those who fear him, from generation to generation. (NIV)

It's my opinion that the best worship songs of today are the ones threaded through with words and phrases from scripture, the living words of God, who wants to communicate his love to us.

Yesterday we saw how Mary's worship song echoes Hannah's song from 1 Samuel. In fact, it also includes echoes of Genesis, Job, Psalms, Esther and Isaiah. Mary knew her Old Testament scriptures and they formed a well of living water from which she drew her outpouring of spontaneous praise.

Mary's words sing out the past mercies of God ('He has performed mighty deeds', v. 51), the present mercies of God ('the Mighty One has done great things for me', v. 49) and the confident hope of his future mercies, 'from generation to generation' (v. 50). She understands that God's plan turns worldly values upside down: a peasant girl will give birth to the King of kings; the humble are the truly great; the poor are more likely to be satisfied than the rich.

As Mary sings, her heart thrills with the certainty that her God, who promised throughout the Old Testament that one day a Saviour would come, is about to fulfil his promise through the baby she carries. No wonder she nearly bursts with praise. For the rest of her pregnancy, Mary must have been sustained by this Holy Spirit-given confidence—and how much she must have needed it, as she and Joseph were forced on the long wearisome journey, dictated by a power-crazy Caesar, from Nazareth to Bethlehem.

Today, Christmas Eve, in millions of households, presents lie in their gaudy paper ready to be revealed tomorrow. Two thousand years ago in Bethlehem, a girl went into labour, ready for God himself to be revealed—in a baby, in a stable.

Lord, thank you for your past, present and future mercies to me. Help me to see Jesus revealed in his word and in my life.

JILL RATTLE

He's here! Happy Christmas!

I bring you good news that will cause great joy for all the people. Today in the town of David a Saviour has been born to you; he is the Messiah, the Lord. (NIV)

I was on Fareham station when the call came: 'You have a granddaughter!' 'Yes!' I shouted, so loudly that heads turned further down the platform. Joy!

I was expecting news of a birth, but the shepherds certainly weren't. One moment you're doing a boring and rather cold night shift with the sheep and the next there is an explosion of light, and an angelic being (busy Gabriel again?) is telling you the most momentous news ever. Seconds later, as if heaven couldn't contain it, an enormous choir of angels bursts forth to join the soloist: 'Glory to God in the highest heaven, and on earth peace to those on whom his favour rests' (v. 14). What? Wow!

The concert halls of the world have never heard more wonderful music than this—and the audience was a bunch of shepherds. Of course, it would be shepherds, wouldn't it? The Bible is just full of shepherds. Many of the Old Testament characters tended flocks of sheep—Abraham, Jacob, Moses in exile and, of course, David, the shepherd-boy made king. Above all, woven into the scriptures is the image of God himself as shepherd of his people. David writes, 'The Lord is my shepherd' (Psalm 23:1). Why? Because a shepherd guides, protects and cares for his sheep. Sheep need a shepherd.

The prophet Micaiah said, 'I saw all Israel scattered on the hills like sheep without a shepherd' (1 Kings 22:17). Generations later, Matthew would echo these words, describing how 'when Jesus saw the crowds, he had compassion on them, because they were harassed and helpless, like sheep without a shepherd' (Matthew 9:36).

The shepherds rushed down from the Bethlehem hill to find a tiny baby who would become the great shepherd and give his life for his sheep.

I hope you are not feeling 'harassed and helpless' today, but, if you are and whenever you are, you have a shepherd who guides, protects and cares for you. Stick close to him.

JILL RATTLE

The angels' song

'Glory to God in the highest heaven, and on earth peace to those on whom his favour rests.' (NIV)

What do you imagine the heavenly choir sounded like? 'Don't think much of the tune,' the shepherds grumble as the angelic band leaves the sky-stage. 'Don't like these modern worship songs,' one mutters; 'too repetitive for me.'

No, of course they didn't stop to criticise the song. All the shepherds knew was that they had experienced worship such as they had never known, and it galvanised them into action. They were in a hurry to see the wonder that the angel had told them about. Perhaps, though, we can pause for a moment and consider the message of the song. The two key words are 'glory' and 'peace'.

The angels knew the glory of God. They dwelt within it, their spiritual beings suffused and energised by it, their very existence dependent on it. They also knew God's amazing plan. The veil between heaven and earth was being breached: the glory of God had touched earth in the form of a tiny human baby, Jesus. The kingdom of heaven had begun to be established on earth, and with it came the possibility of real peace for men and women—not the worldly peace being enjoyed throughout the Roman empire at this point in history, but divine peace, peace with God and the peace of God.

The glory and the peace are inextricably linked. The angels sing, 'Peace to those on whom his favour rests.' Does this mean that God is partial as to whom he blesses with peace? Not at all. The peace is offered to all, but it is dependent on each individual's recognition of 'God's glory displayed in the face of Christ' (2 Corinthians 4:6).

The shepherds saw God in Jesus; their lives were transformed and they became witnesses to the truth of the angels' message.

Use your imagination to sit for a few minutes with the shepherds on the hillside. Hear again the angelic message and song, and let them lead you to Jesus.

JILL RATTLE

Simeon

'Sovereign Lord, as you have promised, you may now dismiss your servant in peace. For my eyes have seen your salvation, which you have prepared in the sight of all nations: a light for revelation to the Gentiles, and the glory of your people Israel.' (NIV)

Two men called John, one called Cecil and one Peter, all four known to me, all lived to old age, continually loving, serving and obeying God and passing on the good news about Jesus. I am so grateful I had them in my life. They remind me of Simeon. I love this old man. He has spent a lifetime praying and expecting God to act. There has been an itch of dissatisfaction in his soul, keeping him watching and waiting, knowing his life's work is not yet complete. The Holy Spirit has revealed to him that he will see the promised Messiah in his lifetime.

Then, on a particular day, at a particular time, the Spirit prompts him to go into the temple. There he sees a young mother carrying a baby. As his eyes fall on the baby, the Spirit within him cries out: 'This is he—this is the promised Saviour not just of the Jews but of the world.' Simeon, like Elizabeth and Mary earlier, lifts up a song of worship—but his song has a bittersweet edge to it, as he prophesies that this baby will be a light to reveal the darkness in the world, darkness that will cut Mary's heart to the quick. Now Simeon's life is complete: he is ready to 'depart in peace' (v. 29). He has fulfilled his mission.

Do you, like me, sometimes feel an itch of dissatisfaction that there must be 'more to come than this'? I believe that God has created us with a holy dissatisfaction that makes us go on seeking and exploring him all our lives. Only at the moment when we encounter Jesus on the other side of death will we say, 'This is it! *This* is what I've been waiting for.'

Are there saints in your life, of advanced years, who inspire you with their faithfulness, love and service? Have you found a way to express your gratitude to them?

JILL RATTLE

Anna

Anna... never left the temple but worshipped night and day, fasting and praying. (NIV)

I had lunch a while back with a former pupil who had just retired as a secondary headteacher. Ouch! I felt my age. To rub it in, small grandchildren seem to have an overkeen interest in the ageing process: 'Grandma, you get older and older and then you die, don't you?' Um, yes. 'Your neck's dying, Grandma!' Thanks!

Well, my body may be showing its age but I really don't want my faith to grow old and saggy with it. I want my faith to be like Anna's. Anna is marvellous. She has suffered the loneliness of widowhood for many years but has devoted herself to worshipping and serving God and praying, praying, praying. She may be old, but she is alive and vibrant with faith. And why shouldn't she be? She is filled with the Holy Spirit, and the Spirit does not age or change. She has been given the gift of prophecy in full measure and her greatest moment of revelation comes when she sees Simeon holding a baby. She knows immediately who this baby is. She rushes up and calls out thanks to God for this miracle, and, having met the baby Jesus, she can't stop telling everyone she meets that the Messiah has come.

As we get older, there is a danger that we may think our usefulness to God is fading. No. No. No. We may no longer do marathons or climb mountains (I never did!) but our spiritual life and service can grow stronger, not weaker. The Holy Spirit is no respecter of age; he gives his gifts to young and old alike—wisdom, prophecy, discernment and all the rest. Older Christians should be the real prayer warriors of the church, working with the Holy Spirit to release power and grace on his people.

Whatever age you are, this is a great prayer: 'Even when I am old and grey, do not forsake me, my God, till I declare your power to the next generation' (Psalm 71:18).

JILL RATTLE

Three (or more?) wise men

When they saw the star, they were overjoyed. On coming to the house, they saw the child with his mother Mary, and they bowed down and worshipped him. (NIV)

For some years I accompanied my scientist husband to a series of weekend 'consultations' on science and faith, held at Windsor Castle. There were some scarily clever people there and phrases like 'anthropic principle', 'neo-Darwinism' and 'ontological anxiety' were tossed about like confetti. It was a relief to get back on Monday to investigating graffiti in the girls' toilets in the school where I worked. What was great, though, was that most of those clever people were followers of Jesus who acknowledged that while science answers many of the 'how?' questions of life, it is faith that answers the 'why?'

The magi, brilliant intellectuals of their day—through research, reasoning and, it must be said, revelation—set out on a long journey to find and worship the 'one who has been born king of the Jews' (v. 2). Unfortunately, at one point their reasoning overtook their faith and diverted them to Herod's palace (the rational place for a king to be born), with dire consequences for the families of Bethlehem. But at last they allowed themselves to be led to a house there, where they fell on their knees, laying down all their cleverness and importance before a small child on his mother's lap, and worshipped.

It's noteworthy that uneducated shepherds were well ahead of the clever magi in finding Jesus. The magi had a much more complex journey than the simple route taken by the shepherds, but the important thing is that they all got there and they all worshipped him in humility.

Today people still come to Jesus by different routes. Some need to go through a complex reasoning process to assure themselves that faith is rational; and, if their minds are open, they will find Jesus. Others come to him with fewer questions and a simpler faith—but there comes a point when we all need to kneel and worship.

Lord, I lay down at your feet all that I am and all you have given me, and I worship you.

JILL RATTLE

Down and down and down

He made himself nothing by taking the very nature of a servant, being made in human likeness. (NIV)

Earlier this month, Diana Archer wrote on this passage. I'd like to revisit it from my own perspective.

When I stepped down as a headteacher, I felt keenly the loss of status. For years I had been an 'important' person in my own small pond, accorded respect and acknowledged as a leader. Now what was I? Some weeks into retirement I found myself, as a member of my church catering team, dressed in a horrible nylon tabard and serving tea to a former colleague. I felt diminished and a bit humiliated. It took me some time to get to the point where I saw that my status, my purpose and my worth were not in a job or role but in my relationship with my Sovereign God. (I'm still working on it!)

Just look at Jesus: co-equal with Father and Spirit; the Creator of all that was, is and will be; the Word; the great 'I Am'. He, Jesus, for love of you and me, stepped down and down and down, confining his divinity within the body of a helpless baby. Then he sank, lower and lower, to a place of humiliation, degradation and disgrace—death on a cross. He 'did not consider equality with God something to be used to his own advantage' (v. 6). He didn't hold on to his status, his dignity or his rights; he willingly gave them up to rescue us.

Someone once helpfully drew for me a distinction between 'choosing to serve' and 'choosing to be a servant'. Many Christians 'choose to serve', choosing when and where and for how long to serve, and reserving the right to withdraw service if it proves too difficult, unappreciated or opposed. A few choose to be servants—in for the duration, taking the rough with the smooth, living in obedience to God wherever it takes them. That was Jesus' choice, to be the servant king.

Are you willing to be the servant of the Servant? That way lies the greatest joy and freedom you can ever know.

JILL RATTLE

It all depends on him

Through him all things were made; without him nothing was made that has been made. (NIV)

My Facebook newsfeed often shows photos of new babies that parents and grandparents have posted, celebrating the beginning of a life that holds infinite possibilities. These babies have come into the world with no prior history, an open book with no words yet written there.

Not so the baby Jesus. As we gaze at the baby in the manger, incredibly we see both man and God. John opens his Gospel by telling us that this baby is 'the Word': Jesus is the full, final, definitive message of God to the world. Jesus' birth was not his beginning: 'In the beginning was the Word, and the Word was with God, and the Word was God' (v. 1). This Word, this Jesus, was co-equal with the Father in the Godhead before creation began. When the galaxies were called into existence, it was through the eternal power of Jesus: everything and everyone, without exception, exists because of Jesus. All life, all light, all power, all love are encompassed in the tiny frame of the baby of Bethlehem.

'*Everything* got started in him and finds its purpose in him. He was there before any of it came into existence and holds it all together right up to this moment' (Colossians 1:16–17, *The Message*). Sometimes it seems our world is falling apart, our society damaged beyond repair, our personal world chaotic and broken. But be assured: 'The Life-Light blazed out of the darkness; the darkness couldn't put it out' (John 1:5, *The Message*).

Revelation 19 has a vision of Jesus' second coming—so different from his first—as the heavenly warrior defeating all evil: 'He is dressed in a robe dipped in blood, and his name is the Word of God' (19:13). We can trust that ultimately Jesus is holding it all, including us, in his hands. We need not be afraid.

Thank you, Lord Jesus, that you broke into history to save us, to save me. Thank you that you hold everything, and me, in your hands—and that one day you will return to complete your divine plan of love.

JILL RATTLE

Recommended reading

ESTHER TAYLOR

Lighted Windows

An Advent calendar for a world in waiting

MARGARET SILF

pb, 9780857464323, £7.99

From the bestselling author Margaret Silf, this new, updated edition of *Lighted Windows* offers readings, reflections and prayers or points for meditation for every day from 1 December to 6 January (Epiphany). The book is based on the theme of looking through the 'windows' of human experience to discover more about God and his call to men and women to follow him. It is also a testimony to the power of waiting—as people wait for Christmas through the Advent season, and as the birth of Messiah was awaited through the centuries. Waiting can be difficult at times, but Christmas proves the value of patience and of taking time to stop, to look out, to listen.

Margaret Silf is an ecumenical Christian, committed to working across and beyond the denominational divides. After working in the computer industry, she left to devote herself to writing in the area of Christian spirituality. Her previous books include *Landmarks—an Ignatian Journey*, *Taste and See—Adventuring into Prayer*, *Wayfaring—A Gospel Journey into Life* (all published by DLT) and *Sacred Spaces—Stations on a Celtic Way* (Lion).

Heaven's Morning

Rethinking the destination

DAVID WINTER

pb, 9780857464767, £7.99

The Bible, especially the New Testament, has plenty to say about resurrection and heaven, but what does it actually mean in practice? David Winter's *Heaven's Morning* explores the biblical teaching on what happens after death and considers what difference this can make to our lives, day by day. Winter, one of the UK's most celebrated Christian authors, proves that eternity can be an empowering source of hope to our sceptical, anxious world, and clarifies what is waiting for us—just beyond.

David Winter is one of the UK's most popular and long established Christian writers and broadcasters. He has written many books over the last 60 years, including *At the End of the Day*, *Facing the Darkness*, *Finding the Light* and *Journey to Jerusalem* for BRF. He also writes for *New Daylight* and contributed regularly to Radio 4's *Thought for the Day* from 1989 to 2012.

St Aidan's Way of Mission

Celtic insights for a post-Christian world

RAY SIMPSON with BRENT LYONS-LEE

pb, 9780857464859, £7.99

Surveying the life and times of Aidan of Lindisfarne, this book brings great insight not only into the character of this complex Celtic man but also into missional approaches that can inspire outreach and discipleship for today's church. As in his previous BRF book, *Hilda of Whitby*, Ray Simpson shows that such figures from past centuries can provide models for Christian life and witness today. Using a combination of historical fact and spiritual teaching, he introduces St Aidan more fully than ever before.

Revd Ray Simpson is a founder of the international new monastic movement known as The Community of Aidan and Hilda and is principal tutor of its Celtic Christian Studies programmes. He has written more than 30 books on spirituality and lives on the island of Lindisfarne, offering a ministry of counsel and support to visitors, especially those in church leadership. He leads retreats on several continents.

Revd Brent Lyons-Lee contributes material from an Australian cross-cultural mission perspective. He is part of the Baptist Union Mission Catalyst team (Victoria, Australia) and a member of The Community of Aidan and Hilda, and has co-written with Ray a book that explores indigenous mission in Australia: *Celtic Spirituality in an Australian Landscape* (St Aidan Press).

Confidence in the Living God

David and Goliath revisited

ANDREW WATSON

pb, 9780857464828, £7.99

Confidence lies at the heart of society, determining the success or failure of the economy, the government, companies, schools, churches and individuals. As Christians, we are called to proclaim our faith in God, but how can we build and maintain this confidence in an increasingly secularised culture where such faith is often seen as marginal, embarrassing or even downright dangerous?

Using the story of David and Goliath as his starting point, Andrew Watson shows how the Lord can indeed be our confidence, whatever the odds. The book includes a discussion guide and is ideal as a whole-church course on the subject of confidence.

Andrew Watson is Bishop of Guildford and author of *The Fourfold Leadership of Jesus* and *The Way of the Desert*, a BRF Lent book. He was previously Bishop of Aston and vicar of St Stephen's, East Twickenham, where he helped pioneer three church plants.

BRF PUBLICATIONS ORDER FORM

To order our resources online, please visit www.brfonline.org.uk

All of these publications are available from Christian bookshops everywhere or, in case of difficulty, direct from the publisher.

Please send me the following book(s):	Quantity	Price	Total
432 3 **Lighted Windows** Margaret Silf	____	£7.99	____
476 7 **Heaven's Morning** David Winter	____	£7.99	____
485 9 **St Aidan's Way of Mission** Ray Simpson	____	£7.99	____
482 8 **Confidence in the Living God** Andrew Watson	____	£7.99	____

POSTAGE AND PACKING CHARGES

Order value	UK	Europe	Rest of World
Under £7.00	£1.25	£3.00	£5.50
£7.00–£29.99	£2.25	£5.50	£10.00
£30.00 & over	FREE	Prices on request	

Total cost of books £ ________

Donation £ ________

Postage and packing £ ________

TOTAL £ ________

Account no. ____________________

Title ______ First name/initials ________ Surname ______________

Address ____

______________________________ Postcode ______________

Telephone ______________ Email ____________________________

Total enclosed £ __________ (cheques should be made payable to 'BRF')

Please charge my Mastercard ☐ Visa ☐ Debit card ☐ with £ __________

Card no. ☐☐☐☐ ☐☐☐☐ ☐☐☐☐ ☐☐☐☐

Valid from M M Y Y Expires M M Y Y

Security code* ☐☐☐ **Last 3 digits on the reverse of the card*
ESSENTIAL IN ORDER TO PROCESS YOUR ORDER

Signature ______________________________ Date ___ /___ /___
(essential if paying by credit card)

To read our terms and find out about cancelling your order, please visit www.brfonline.org.uk/terms

Please send your completed form with the appropriate payment to:
BRF, 15 The Chambers, Vineyard, Abingdon OX14 3FE

The Bible Reading Fellowship (BRF) is a Registered Charity (233280). VAT No: GB 238 5574 35

DAY BY DAY WITH GOD: SUBSCRIPTION INFORMATION

Each issue of **Day by Day with God** is available from Christian bookshops everywhere. Copies may also be available through your church book agent or from the person who distributes Bible reading notes in your church.

Alternatively you may obtain **Day by Day with God** on subscription direct from the publishers. There are two kinds of subscription:

Individual subscriptions
covering 3 issues for 4 copies or less, payable in advance (including postage & packing).

To order, please complete the details on page 144 and return with the appropriate payment to: BRF, 15 The Chambers, Vineyard, Abingdon OX14 3FE

You can also use the form on page 144 to order a gift subscription for a friend.

Church subscriptions
covering 3 issues for 5 copies or more, sent to **one** UK address (post free).

Please note that the annual billing period for church subscriptions runs from 1 May to 30 April.

To order, please complete the details on page 143 and return with the appropriate payment to: BRF, 15 The Chambers, Vineyard, Abingdon OX14 3FE

You will receive an invoice with the first issue of notes.

All our Bible reading notes can be ordered online by visiting
www.biblereadingnotes.org.uk/subscriptions

For information about our other Bible reading notes, and apps for iPhone and iPod touch, visit
www.biblereadingnotes.org.uk

All subscription enquiries should be directed to:
BRF, 15 The Chambers, Vineyard, Abingdon OX14 3FE
Tel: 01865 319700 | Fax: 01865 319701 | email: enquiries@brf.org.uk

DAY BY DAY WITH GOD: CHURCH SUBSCRIPTION FORM

All our Bible reading notes can be ordered online by visiting
www.biblereadingnotes.org.uk/subscriptions

The church subscription rate for **Day by Day with God** will be £13.05 per person until April 2017.

☐ I would like to take out a church subscription for ______ (quantity) copies.

☐ Please start my order with the January 2017/May 2017/September 2017* issue. I would like to pay annually/receive an invoice with each edition of the notes*. (**delete as appropriate*)

Please do not send any money with your order. Send your order to BRF and we will send you an invoice. The church subscription year is from 1 May to 30 April. If you start subscribing in the middle of a subscription year we will invoice you for the remaining number of issues left in that year.

Name and address of the person organising the church subscription:

Title ______ First name/initials ______ Surname ____________________

Address ____

____ Postcode ____________

Telephone ______________ Email ____________________________

Church ____

Name of Minister ____

Name and address of the person paying the invoice if the invoice needs to be sent directly to them:

Title ______ First name/initials ______ Surname ____________________

Address ____

____ Postcode ____________

Telephone ______________ Email ____________________________

Please return this completed form to:
BRF, 15 The Chambers, Vineyard, Abingdon OX14 3FE

DAY BY DAY WITH GOD: INDIVIDUAL/GIFT SUBSCRIPTION FORM

To order online, please visit **www.biblereadingnotes.org.uk/subscriptions**

☐ **I would like to give a gift subscription** (please provide both names and addresses)

☐ **I would like to take out a subscription myself** (complete your name and address details only once)

Title ________ First name/initials ________ Surname ____________________

Address ____

______________________________ Postcode ____________

Telephone ______________ Email ______________________

Gift subscription name ______________________________

Gift subscription address ____________________________

______________________________ Postcode ____________

Gift message (20 words max. or include your own gift card):

____

____

Please send Day by Day with God beginning with the January 2017/May 2017/ September 2017 issue (*delete as appropriate*):

(*please tick box*)	**UK**	**Europe**	**Rest of World**
Day by Day with God	☐ £16.35	☐ £24.00	☐ £27.60
2-year subscription	☐ £28.50	N/A	N/A

Total enclosed £ __________ (cheques should be made payable to 'BRF')

Please charge my Mastercard ☐ Visa ☐ Debit card ☐ with £ __________

Card no. ☐☐☐☐ ☐☐☐☐ ☐☐☐☐ ☐☐☐☐

Valid from M M Y Y Expires M M Y Y

Security code* ☐☐☐ **Last 3 digits on the reverse of the card*
ESSENTIAL IN ORDER TO PROCESS YOUR ORDER

Signature ______________________________ Date ___/___/___

(essential if paying by credit card)

To read our terms and find out about cancelling your order, please visit www.brfonline.org.uk/terms

To set up a Direct Debit, please also complete the Direct Debit instruction on page 159 and return it to BRF with this form.

Please send your completed form with the appropriate payment to:
BRF, 15 The Chambers, Vineyard, Abingdon OX14 3FE